PET OWNER'S GUIDE TO
DOGS

PET OWNER'S GUIDE TO

DOGS

Kay White

HOWELL BOOK HOUSE INC.
230 Park Avenue, New York, N.Y. 10169

CONTENTS

Published in 1987 by
Howell Book House Inc.
230 Park Avenue, New York, N.Y.10169

Copyright © Nicholas Enterprises Limited
70 Old Compton Street, London W1V 5PA

Library of Congress Cataloging-in-Publication Data

White, Kay.
    Pet owners' guide to dogs.

    Summary: A guide to dog ownership including how to select a dog, descriptions of popular breeds, and how to care for a puppy and older dog.
    1. Dogs. [1. Dogs] I. Title.
SF426.W47   1987   636.7   86-27325

ISBN 0-87605-769-5

Chihuahua **32**

Pomeranian **34**

Yorkshire Terrier **35**

Maltese **36**

Bichon Frise **37**

Miniature Pinscher **39**

Pekingese **40**

Miniature
Dachshund **42**

Cavalier King Charles
Spaniel **44**

Border
Terrier **46**

Cairn Terrier **47**

Lhasa Apso **48**

Pug **49**

Shih Tzu **50**

West Highland
White Terrier **52**

Jack Russell
Terrier **53**

Scottish Terrier **54**

Shetland Sheepdog **55**

Miniature Schnauzer **56**

Beagle **58**

Pembroke Welsh Corgi **59**

Boston Terrier **60**

Cocker Spaniel (English and American) **62**

Staffordshire Bull Terrier **64**

Whippet **66**

Australian Cattle Dog **68**

Brittany **69**

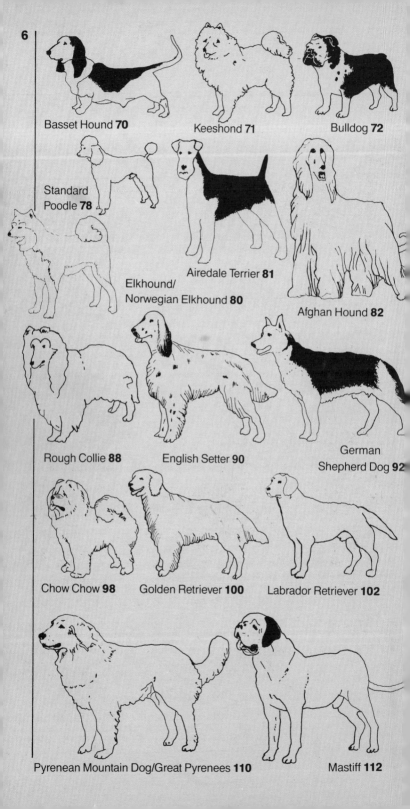

6

Basset Hound **70**

Keeshond **71**

Bulldog **72**

Standard
Poodle **78**

Airedale Terrier **81**

Elkhound/
Norwegian Elkhound **80**

Afghan Hound **82**

Rough Collie **88**

English Setter **90**

German
Shepherd Dog **92**

Chow Chow **98**

Golden Retriever **100**

Labrador Retriever **102**

Pyrenean Mountain Dog/Great Pyrenees **110**

Mastiff **112**

Siberian Husky **74** Samoyed **76** English Springer Spaniel **77**

Dobermann/Doberman Pinscher **84**

Bearded Collie **86**

German
Short-Haired Pointer **87**

Weimaraner **96**

Dalmatian **94**

Boxer **97**

Rottweiler **106**

Japanese Akita/Akita **104**

Old English Sheepdog **108**

St Bernard **116**

Great Dane **114** Newfoundland **118**

Introduction

The relationship between man and dog began more than 10,000 years ago when primitive man and the as yet undomesticated dog realized they could be of use to each other. As a hunter, early man competed for the same prey as canines. Because he was larger, more intelligent and armed with weapons, man was inevitably more successful but he also recognized that the dog's ability to scent and track down prey was superior to his. Dogs could help man and they, in turn, understood that in exchange for their services, they could be fed and protected by a "pack leader" who would efficiently ensure the survival of their species. The relationship was thus an eminently practical one and it is well worth remembering this in an age when the man/dog relationship is influenced by many complex factors.

Dog's fidelity

The dog's fidelity to its human master or mistress is legendary. Unlike the cat, which was domesticated about 5000 years ago, the dog never reverts to life in the wild voluntarily and even when lost or strayed, will usually make some attempt to approach human habitation. The dog's allegiance to man, unique in the animal world, must never be forgotten by the prospective dog owner nor treated lightly. In the modern world, this devotion has sometimes turned the dog into a puzzling creature, not always easy to understand. Some dogs attempt to dominate the humans with which they live. Others have become so integrated with people as to be dangerously aggressive to their own species, or so humanized that they will not mate with their own kind. These unfortunate consequences are, on the whole, the result of poor training and a failure on the part of the pet owner to understand the dog's basic nature.

A dog's life

Our own expansion into a richer, fuller and more complex human existence has lowered the quality of life we can offer dogs. Yet the essentials for a dog's life are relatively simple. They require shelter, food, companionship, plenty of interest and activity to watch or take part in, and a code of reasonable – but unalterable – rules which govern the dog's role within the family, as well as liberal appreciation and approval by its master or mistress when those rules are kept.

Never buy on impulse

Dogs, and puppies especially, are eminently *wantable* and can all too easily be bought on impulse from pet shops and kennels. Sadly, all over the world, young and healthy dogs have to be destroyed because the wanting did not last and the impulse was unwise. Complete, wholehearted agreement in any group of people, even as small as the average family, is difficult, but there are few more disruptive elements within a household than a pet which is unwelcome to one or more family members. Puppies and adult dogs are not easy to live with; they require a measure of tolerance from their human family. There are times when the dog intrudes in our lives in an unwelcome way, when there are places we cannot go to, things we cannot own because we have a dog. A puppy may ruin our treasures, despoil our garden just through sheer exuberance and mischief, but once the dog is disliked by one or other family member, its life as a pet will be intolerable.

A rejected dog joins the ranks of canine failures, unwanted dogs competing for attention and new owners at a dog shelter. Sadly, about half of the puppies bought as pets are doomed to fail. Perhaps the owners bought the wrong kind of dog, one that needed more training and attention than they had time to give. Maybe their lifestyle could not accommodate a dog and they were misled by that fatal puppy-attraction. Whatever the reason, this really should never happen. A dog is a living and intelligent creature which experiences pain and pleasure; its owner must make a lifetime commitment to it – because it is not an inanimate object to be taken up and discarded at will.

Commitment for life

If you are prepared to make that commitment, your relationship can be mutually beneficial and happy. Scientists have pointed out that dogs are good for your health. Generally, people with pets are more stable and less prone to stress than others. Dogs can also supply many needs lacking in human relationships, not least the uncritical affection and tactile response which buffers our ego so well against isolation by our fellow humans. Fidelity and sincerity are the companion dog's greatest virtues and when reciprocated can be a wonderful bonus in an age when so many human relationships are sadly lacking in both.

DOGS PAST AND PRESENT

At the end of the twentieth century, dogs are, in many ways, worse off than ever before in their history. It is true that the majority of dogs are extremely well-fed, and comfortably housed with man rather than in kennels, and in general, dogs are not subjected to deliberate physical cruelty such as was commonplace in the nineteenth century. But in exchange for a life of comparative luxury, dogs have had to give up a great deal of the natural heritage of their kind. They are now the most domesticated and confined of all animals, with the result that many of their instinctive characteristics have been supressed or frustrated.

Dogs' role in the human pack

Dogs are not by nature solitary animals. They need to be part of a pack which is mutually supportive but which is dominated by a pack leader. Most dogs compromise well by becoming part of the human pack or family with which they live. The ambitious dog may still challenge its human owner for superiority, particularly when the owner is uncertain or lacks confidence with dogs or is indulgent. The dog pounds and rescue homes are full of such "failed pets" which were not given an early chance to learn that dogs must always be, in a domestic situation, very near the bottom of the ranking order. Their inherited instincts makes it essential for dogs to have the security of knowing what behaviour is acceptable and what behaviour will bring punishment of a kind which the dog can interpret. Most dogs appreciate a framework of routine and unchanging standards within which they can live.

Special talents and past uses

Dogs also need to exercise the talents for which their kind was developed, be it hunting game by scent or sight, killing vermin, or guarding territory. With the exception of toy dogs, always bred as ladies' pets and comforters, dogs have only survived down the centuries because they were useful to man in some particular way. With relatively few exceptions, we do not need the skills the dog has to offer, so we keep it under employed, perhaps never employed at all. That state, to a healthy, active and well-fed dog is probably more of a cruelty than we realize.

Dogs have much better hearing than man, and can recognize and follow scents which are unknown to man. They can run faster, and for longer, and they bring their old pack habits into use by working well as a team. Man has used these talents from the earliest man/dog associations, first as an aid to hunting for food, a partnership which survives in a limited way today. Dogs also guarded and herded flocks of sheep and drove cattle over long distances to market and, as well, guarded the full purse of money on the way home. From the Middle Ages, toy dogs were kept as companions by aristocratic ladies but even they were allowed more freedom than we offer today. Dogs helped in the home by turning cooking spits and also by killing vermin before there were chemical eradicators. They also provided entertainment, from the troupes of performing Poodles common in the eighteenth century to the battle-scarred warriors who made record killings in the rat pits, or were matched against each other in dog fights.

In the mid-nineteenth century it was not uncommon to provide a spectator sport by matching a pack of dogs against a lion in private zoos, and bullbaiting using the smaller mastiff-type dogs was a common entertainment on feast days in country towns. Newfoundland dogs helped fishermen pull in boats and rescued those who went overboard, and they also turned waterwheels on large estates. During the nineteenth century, dogs were an important means of transporting loads which had to arrive in fresh condition. A mixed team would pull laden carts at great speed, the exhausted dogs being left to die by the roadside at the journey's end.

A completely new use for dogs began in 1859, when the first dog shows were held, with just a handful of dogs being put before a judge. Now dog showing is a universal hobby with some 10,000 dogs being present at shows which are held almost every day in Britain during the summer season. In America, many exhibitors travel the country in specially equipped vehicles with their dogs, moving on from show to show on designated circuits.

New uses for working dogs

A minority of dogs still have work to do, and no one watching them can fail to appreciate how much they enjoy performing a task which they are well equipped for. Some aspects of the dog's work have been extended – for instance, the modern detect and search dogs, trained to find drugs, explosives, or weapons (however, dogs have been found unreliable in

Guide dog for the blind

detecting *other dogs*). Armies and police forces all over the world use dogs as deterrents, guards and attack dogs. Guide dogs for the blind (Seeing Eye dogs) are a twentieth century utilization of the dog's ability to obey and to discriminate between safety and danger, and the dog's hearing, and ability to communicate in its own way with its master is used by hearing dogs for the deaf. We still use dogs, and not only toy dogs, as familiars and comfort objects. Dogs are still an essential element on the shooting field, and if we have no shooting, we enter them in specially staged trials.

Many of the working dogs mentioned have been specially bred to develop physical attributes which enable them to use their skills to the full. All the individuals of the breed or type will have those same skills to some degree. The pet Labrador, which has never heard a gun fired, still has a waterproof coat to protect it from the harsh weather it never sees, and it still has the stamina to run all day over forest and downland, although the extent of its exercise may only be occasional weekend outings. Small wonder that bored and frustrated work-dogs often use their energy destroying the home in which they spend so many lonely hours. It must never be forgotten that a dog's prime needs are for company and activity; these were more readily satisfied in past times than they are perhaps today.

CONSIDERATIONS BEFORE GETTING A DOG

If you are considering getting a dog but have not yet made up your mind, there are a number of practical problems which the prospective dog owner must face. First and foremost, a puppy or an adult dog should never be taken into a home on impulse, whether based on sympathy for a stray dog which needs a home, or from desire to own an attractive and friendly pet. The truth must be faced. *All dogs*, however well-loved, are a nuisance and a burden at times. This is because of their life-long dependency on their owners.

Total dependency on owner

When a puppy is very young, this dependency is part of the attraction, but the adolescent, middle-aged and elderly dog is also dependent upon its owners, not only for food and veterinary care, but for company, entertainment and general care and supervision. Once you have a dog you lose a certain amount of freedom, and it is lost for as long as the dog lives. You must be very sure that what you receive in exchange from the dog is worth what you will lose, otherwise you, or some member of your family, will feel resentment, and eventual dislike for the dog.

Need for constant companionship

It is commonly thought that once puppy days are over a dog will be trouble-free. Yet domestication is merely a thin veneer on top of thousands of years of living wild, and in dogs it can only be maintained by being with human beings for most of every day. Dogs will, of course, live with their own kind in kennels quite happily, but if this is their permanent way of life, such dogs rapidly become less people-orientated. With neglect or lack of constant human companionship, a dog will soon revert to "wild" behaviour which makes it unsuitable for any home. This may take the form of frantic destruction of the owner's house and possessions, compulsive chewing of its own limbs, house-soiling, constant barking, or aggression to other dogs or to humans.

Most of this bad behaviour could be eradicated in puppy days by human companionship and sensible teaching, but if left on its own a puppy or an adult dog will always develop bad behaviour patterns. This need for companionship is, therefore, one of the most important considerations when discussing dog ownership. Even a mature dog should not spend more than four hours a day alone, and a puppy or adolescent not more than one to two hours. Companionship, when given, should be at least as long as the time spent alone. A quick visit of, say 15 minutes and then another four hours alone is not the answer.

Consider your family

It is not enough for one member of the family to be enthusiastic about getting a dog. The whole household must want the dog. Dogs are quick to detect resentment or dislike and this can have a profound effect on their psychological well-being. Any person who could be over-harsh with the dog or over-indulgent may spoil its character. If your household includes children and/or elderly relatives consider too, how a dog will fit in with the established "pecking order" in your family. Can your family take in another member and satisfy its needs? Careful thought must also be given to the choice of breed which should be one which you positively like and want but which also suits your family and its lifestyle.

Dogs and children

A great many dogs make wonderful companions for children, especially when reared from puppyhood in the company of youngsters (older dogs, especially if mistreated in the past, may have a positive dislike of children which only patience and love will overcome). However, it is unwise to acquire a puppy where there are children under five years old. Older children can benefit enormously from owning a dog, provided they are taught good manners towards the dog and are not allowed to exercise powerful dogs on public roads. Small toy breeds are not usually compatible with children.

Consider friends and visitors

Some of your friends will dislike dogs, particularly when they are pawed or jumped on. Do not rely on your dog being perfectly controlled and behaved at all times and be prepared to lose a few friends because of it and to have your social life constrained in some ways. If your household does have a constant stream of visitors, be sure to choose a breed which is not wary of strangers.

Home location – points to remember

- Potentially noisy breeds may annoy close neighbours.
- Medium-sized to large dogs can scale 3 metre (7ft) high walls and wire fences.
- Male dogs may be constantly upset if there are in-season bitches nearby.
- Hounds can dig under fencing.
- Bull breeds and guarding breeds are often unsuitable to exercise in public parks in towns.
- Breeds in which there is prominent inter-male jealousy may be difficult to walk through a town or on the way to an open space.
- Untrained gun dogs should not be exercised where shooting rights are preserved.

Irish Water Spaniel

- Dogs should not be allowed to run free where there are wild deer.
- The water dogs, (Newfoundland, Water Spaniels etc) should have frequent access to freshwater ponds.

Saluki

Size and location of your house

Your house or apartment must be big enough to provide enough space for a dog to live comfortably. Needs vary from breed to breed. Your dog must also be exercised and a large, fenced-in garden or easy access to exercise areas is essential for some breeds. It is particularly important for urban dwellers to consider these needs carefully since some breeds are simply not suited to city or town life. Existing in a confined space or where exercise is difficult will make a miserable life for both owner and dog.

Have you enough time for a dog?

Owning a dog is time-consuming and more so with some breeds than others. All dogs need basic care and attention, such as feeding and exercising, as well as careful training from puppyhood to maturity. Daily activities with a dog are also essential and these can range from vigorous walks and constructive play to extensive grooming. If you lead a busy lifestyle and cannot be actively involved with your dog for the minimum amount of time suggested for exercising and grooming your particular breed, you would be unwise to get a dog.

You can afford a dog?

The dog will be a charge upon your income. The direct costs include food, pet insurance where available, veterinary fees, collars, leads, rugs, beds, toys, boarding kennel fees during vacations, illness of owner or business trips, travel costs, shampoos, grooming equipment, professional trimming and a dog licence.

In a medium to large breed dog, weighing about 29.5kg (65 lbs), needing professional trimming twice a year and boarded for 20 days annually, the cost will be about £400/ $570 per year based on 1987 figures. A puppy in the same breed will cost at least £500/$700 in its first year. A giant breed incurs greater costs in every area, from beds and collars to medication and anaesthetics, and a larger car in which to carry it. The initial cost of buying a purebred puppy varies widely according to market demands but can be, in 1987, anything from £120/$170 to £450/$640 for a top quality puppy. Consider too, a number of indirect costs. Dogs create extra housework because of hair shedding, pawmarks on the floor and body grease on paintwork. Soft furnishings need laundering and replacing more frequently, and cars used for dog transport can seldom be re-sold for a high price. A dog may ruin and spoil a garden, and there may be need for extra fencing and gates, and protection for a swimming pool.

CHOOSING A DOG

Once you have decided to get a dog, you are faced with yet another set of questions to which you must give careful consideration. There is a great deal more to choosing a dog than simply walking into a pet shop or animal shelter and selecting a dog because you like the look of it. You, the would-be owner, must decide not merely what type of dog you want but whether you prefer a puppy or adult dog, male or female or purebred or mongrel.

Puppy or adult?

Ideally, the pet owner should rear his dog from puppyhood. The bond between dog and owner is established at an early age and throughout the dog's growing stage this is likely to be cemented in a mutually happy and satisfying relationship. Remember, however, that a puppy is totally dependent on its owner and needs a lot of time, attention and patience lavished on it. Feeding, toilet training and teaching a puppy good manners cannot be done easily; irritation must also be curbed when accidents occur and when puppies chew everything in sight.

Choosing an older dog, however, is not without problems. Any owner will have to work particularly hard at building up a secure, solid relationship with an older dog, particularly if it is an abandoned or stray animal which may have been ill-treated in the past. You will have difficulty modifying established behaviour patterns and it may take a long time before the dog really accepts and trusts you and your family. Rescuing a dog from loneliness can, however, be especially rewarding when in the end you win its loyalty and affection.

Male or female?

Not only must you decide whether you want a male or female dog, but also whether you want it spayed or castrated. There is no doubt that desexed dogs and bitches make them more tolerable pets but if you wish to breed from your dog, this is not an option.

Male dog: Among the disadvantages of the uncastrated male are that it will use shrubs, posts and fences for territory marking (by leaving small squirts of urine) and may mark curtains and doors if another dog or bitch has visited the house; it will be restless, disobedient and wandering when female dogs in the neighbourhood are in heat; it displays overt sexual behaviour at adolescence (but usually settles down thereafter); and in general it is probably more difficult to control than a bitch and more aggressive with other dogs. On the plus side, it is usually more consistent in character, with fewer mood swings than the bitch.

Bitch: The unspayed bitch generally has a softer, more biddable character than the male and is thus easier to control. However, the major disadvantage is the bitch's oestrus periods (in heat) which occur every 6-10 months. During this time the dog is restless and unreliable, her "spotting" can make a mess of your home and exercise has to be restricted. Following oestrus, all bitches have, in some degree, a false or phantom pregnancy when they carry, give birth to and suckle imaginary puppies. For some bitches, this can be a very disturbing experience which temporarily alters the character of the dog. All of this can be very trying for the owner yet it is precisely in these difficult times that the bitch needs maximum care and understanding.

Advantages of desexing: Spaying or sterilization of the bitch is a routine operation in which the ovaries and uterus are removed. This should be done at about six to nine months or as soon as possible after the dog has reached physical maturity (which varies from breed to breed). For urban or suburban owners, spaying really is advisable. It is kinder to the animal and also makes its owner's life much easier. Dogs can be castrated in a relatively cheap operation which involves the removal of the testicles. It is usually performed when the dog is over a year old, recovery is rapid but the effects may not be seen for up to six months. This is again advisable for urban and suburban pet owners, although it is not generally as routine a procedure as spaying. The most forceful reasons for desexing dogs and bitches is that there are far too many unwanted animals everywhere and any move that can reduce the number of these unloved and pathetic creatures is to be encouraged. Desexing generally produces better and more placid house pets. However, with some guard dogs, hunting and working breeds, the minor behavioural changes which occur with desexing can alter their performance or working ability. In these cases, it is best to seek veterinary advice before desexing.

Junior handling class with purebred Afghans outside show ring.

Purebred, crossbred or mongrel?

Before choosing a purebred dog, carefully read *Popular Dog Breeds* (pages 22-119) which gives basic information about the breed, as well as noting its good and bad points.

Purebred dogs: A purebred dog has at least four generations of only one breed of dog in its pedigree. Registration by a kennel club serves in part to check this, although until positive identification of puppies by tattooed and registered numbers becomes the custom, there is no way to positively relate a purebred dog to its pedigree. There may be "throwbacks" in any purebred litter which are odd by colour, size, coat type or conformation, but in general the purebred pup will resemble its forebears in all its attributes. Individual temperaments will always vary within a litter, and character tendencies will be magnified or lessened according to the environment into which the puppy goes.

Many purebred dogs are bred to close relations in order to improve the quality of their offspring. Known as inbreeding and linebreeding, these methods can intensify bad points as well, and may increase the tendency towards hereditary diseases.

All kennel clubs demand that dogs must be registered before they can enter all but the most informal shows. Registration formality demands that one or more generations of parents are also registered, so this is something a buyer must check if he wants to enter the show ring or to breed puppies for show purposes.

Mongrel, a gamble for pet ownership

Crossbreds: This dog is the result of a mating between two purebred individuals of different breeds, perhaps because of a kennel accident or as a deliberate outcross to bring new blood into an established breed. In Britain, for example, improved guide dogs for the blind have been deliberately produced by cross breeding between Labrador and Golden Retriever. Accidental crosses are not always so successful, since the attributes of two purebred dogs may not harmonize. A guard dog/gundog cross, for example, is likely to produce a neurotic dog, uncertain of its role by being too quarrelsome with other dogs for gun work but too gregarious with humans to guard. In fact, accidental crosses are just as much a lottery as mongrels and should only be taken on with full awareness of the problems involved.

Mongrels: These are the dogs of unknown ancestry which usually fill the rescue homes and dog pounds of the world. They can be very appealing and many make fine pets but the mongrel is always a gamble for pet ownership. It is a myth that mongrels are more hardy than purebred dogs. In fact, it is probable that there is a high degree of inbreeding in mongrels since they are likely to mate with dogs in their neighbourhood which may, in turn, be closely related. Also neither the parents nor the litter will have been given the specialized care afforded to purebred stock.

Most mongrels are acquired as puppies or young adults from dog shelters and the dog's true character will only be revealed after a few weeks. Be warned: many mongrels are born wanderers, impossible to keep within fences while others can be wilful, excitable and noisy. Mongrels should be vaccinated immediately they are acquired and thereafter, trained, groomed and cared for in every way like their purebred cousins.

Non-pedigree dogs: In Great Britain, there are two types of non-pedigree dogs which have become especially popular in recent years although they are not recognized by the British Kennel Club. There is a great deal of size and coat variation in the favoured Jack Russell Terrier and this has prevented Kennel Club recognition, much to the chagrin of some of its devoted owners. It is usually an independent, self-reliant little dog, adept at disturbing other animals, a good ratter, and a quick snapper. Lurchers, another popular breed, are usually from Greyhounds crossed with a large terrier. Traditionally poacher's dogs, they combine running speed with quick killing ability but they can be great trouble to their owner because of their tendency to kill cats and other small domestic pets.

Where to buy a dog

There are a number of ways you can acquire a dog – most commonly from pet shops, breeders and dog pounds or shelters. Regardless of the potential source of your dog, take a careful look at the animals and their general state of health and well-being as well as the surroundings. As with all things, some breeders are very reputable and others should be shunned; some pet shops offer fine, healthy puppies and others are not as conscientious. It's definitely a grey area. Talk to the person in charge about the breeds you are considering and discuss the pros and cons of the breeds, including health problems. All reputable sellers should talk frankly with you and this will help you make your choice. Remember, however, that you should *never* buy on impulse. Think carefully about your choice before deciding to buy an animal.

All these preliminary investigations are necessary since you are, after all, choosing a long-term companion. When finally your choice of breed has been made and you come to choose a particular puppy, you will be more confident about what you want.

POPULAR DOG BREEDS

In the following section of this book, the most popular breeds of dog worldwide are described, with comments on their virtues and drawbacks as well as the type of home and/or owners to which they are most suited. This is by no means a definitive list of dog breeds, which is impossible in a book of this size, but it is to be hoped that the observations here will be useful not only to the first-time buyer but also to those who already own a dog and to those who are interested in dogs and their characteristics. The comments are based on the author's life-long experience with dogs and, inevitably, many pet owners and dog lovers may disagree with them because they have never encountered some of the less pleasant traits mentioned. However, it is essential for people who own a dog, or are intending to get one, to be aware of *potential* problems in the breed they have chosen, whether it be a possible hereditary illness or a fault or quirk of temperament. Buyers of a new puppy should certainly check for these, if possible, in the parents of the litter when a purchase is considered.

Consider your character and lifestyle

It is, of course, impossible to prescribe a dog for another person, or even to choose a dog for oneself from a written description. Obviously, a successful pet/owner relationship depends on the owner's strong attraction to either the appearance or characteristics of the breed, or both. It is also necessary for the owner to come to terms with his or her own character and lifestyle, and to estimate fairly the amount of time which is available to spend on teaching, grooming, exercising and giving companionship to the dog. It must always be remembered that the dog is a pack animal, and if its life is to be with a human family, it must be around the animal for much of the day and night. Few dogs are happy for many hours alone and some will become neurotic and self-destructive, if bored and lonely.

The need for daily exercise is a year-long activity in nearly all breeds and dogs prefer daylight exercise. The dog owner should think not only of sunny weekends, but should picture the worst weather, the busiest social commitments, the fewest helpers and the lowest income within his personal range. If the dog will fit into that lifestyle, then it will fit into better conditions as well.

Two dogs or one?

Many first-time owners feel it removes some of the commitments of ownership if they take two puppies, but this is rarely successful. Two pups of the same age will be difficult to housetrain, and will always be more devoted to each other than to their owners. However, if you already have a dog and are considering another, or if you definitely want two dogs, wait until the first puppy is six months old before getting the dog. Small, non-aggressive breeds will accept an adult newcomer but possessive dogs with a strong sense of territory will strongly resent a new adult, although they will admit a puppy. Two bitches, or a dog and a bitch, are the best choice. Two males of the guarding or aggressive breeds are a bad choice since they are liable to fight for pack leadership. If a dog and bitch is chosen, either one or both must be neutered as it is virtually impossible to keep both animals in the same house when the bitch is in heat, unless, of course, you plan to breed.

Problems with some breeds

If you have chosen a breed as a companion dog, consider its instinctive characteristics established over many generations. Certain sight hounds, particularly the Saluki and Afghan, may never be able to be let off the lead, since these breeds are very poor at responding to recall. Gundogs should not be exercised where they can chase game. Fighting breeds, particularly types of Bull Terrier, may be difficult to exercise in urban areas because of their habit of picking quarrels with passing dogs. Toy breeds are at risk where there are boisterous children. Giant breeds such as the Great Dane and St Bernard need spacious accommodation (including in a car), cost more to feed, outfit with collars and beds, and more for veterinary attention and for boarding during the owner's absence. Long-coated breeds and many others require daily grooming so you must consider where this is to be done, particularly in the winter months.

Guard dogs

The German Shepherd Dog, Rottweiler, Boxer, Bull Mastiff and Bull Terrier need no training in guarding duties and it is extremely dangerous to try to improve on their natural instincts, which do not usually show until the dog is about two years old. Guard dogs should never be chained up; this can make the dog unpredictably savage to all within its reach or so frustrated that it may lose its guard instinct.

It is essential to train a guard dog to stop on command and, even if this is the only command it ever knows, it may save the dog's life and, more importantly, that of an innocent human. Guard breeds are not suited to homes which have a constant stream of visitors. They can sometimes misinterpret the actions of well-meaning people, especially those who wave their arms in extravagant gestures, which to the dog may seem a threat to its owner or family members. They can also react badly to shrill cries by children if unused to this sound and may attack people taking an innocent stroll around your property. Guard dogs are often friendly to visitors while they are seated but show aggression if the visitor stands up, touches household possessions or attempts to move from room to room in its owner's absence. Like humans and other dogs, even the best-trained guard dog can make a mistake – which can have tragic results. Think very carefully before you choose a guard breed as a pet. Remember that there are many casual, everyday situations to which this dog should not be exposed and it is the owner's responsibility to make sure it is not.

Sizes and descriptions

The breeds listed below are arranged, approximately, in order of increasing weight (even though the KC or AKC breed standards do not always specify weight). The height and weight given in the description is that of the adult male according to KC or AKC breed standards. A rough guide to the size of the puppy can be deduced from these. Requirements for the show ring are detailed and specific, and owners intent on showing should make a thorough study of the appropriate breed standard before buying a puppy.

Height is measured to the withers (the point where the neck meets the back). Overall, the dog will appear taller when carrying the head high. Bitches are generally a little shorter in height and 4.5-6.8kg (10-15 lbs) lighter in most breeds unless otherwise specified.

German Shepherd Dog

POPULAR DOG BREEDS: RATINGS CHART

The chart below shows at a glance the major characteristics of the 58 breeds discussed. Use this as a guide to the types of dog best suited to your housing/living conditions and to your lifestyle.

BREED	EXERCISE			GROOMING			HUNTING ABILITY
	Minimal	Average	Extensive	Minimal	Average	Extensive	
Chihuahua	■			■			
Pomeranian	■					■	
Yorkshire Terrier		■				■	
Maltese		■				■	
Bichon Frise		■		■			■
Miniature Pinscher		■				■	
Pekingese	■					■	
Miniature Dachshund		■			■		■
Cavalier King Charles Spaniel		■			■		■
Border Terrier		■		■			■
Cairn Terrier		■		■			■
Lhasa Apso		■				■	
Pug	■			■			
Shih Tzu		■				■	
West Highland White Terrier		■			■		■
Jack Russell Terrier		■		■			■
Scottish Terrier		■			■		■

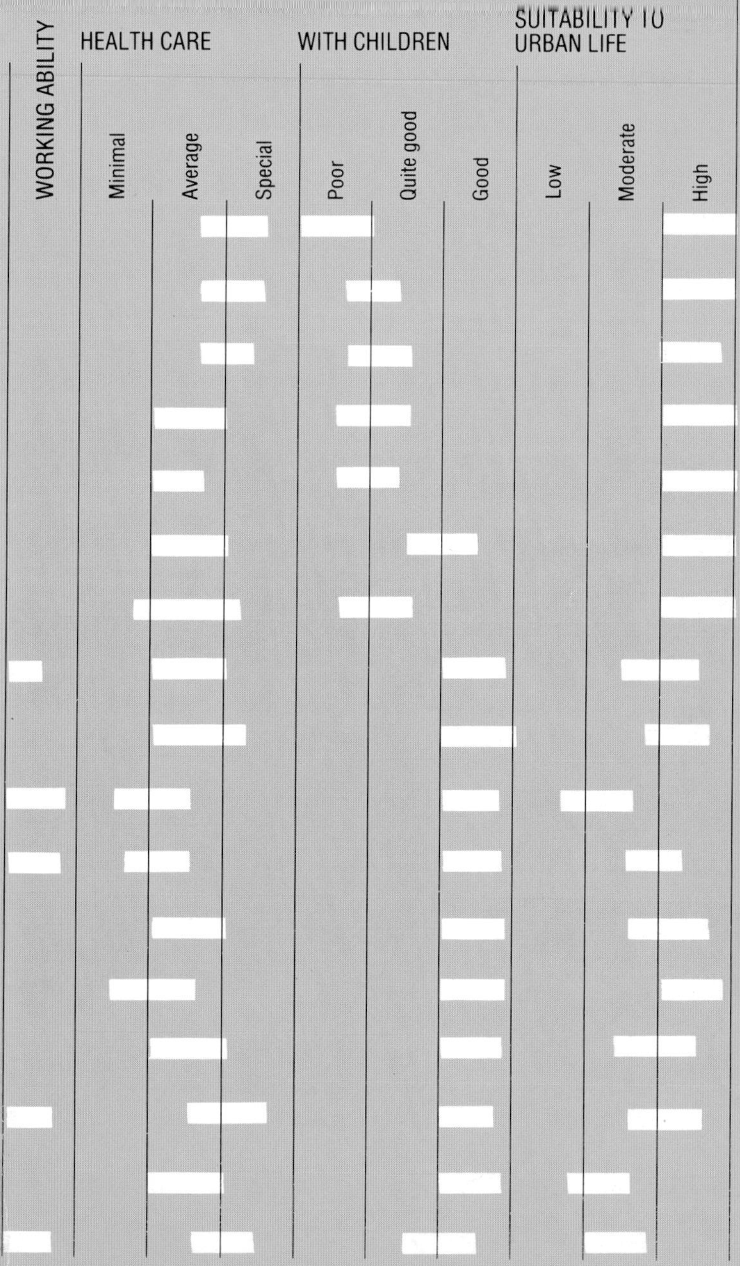

WORKING ABILITY
HEALTH CARE
Minimal
Average
Special
WITH CHILDREN
Poor
Quite good
Good
SUITABILITY TO URBAN LIFE
Low
Moderate
High

BREED	EXERCISE			GROOMING			HUNTING ABILITY
	Minimal	Average	Extensive	Minimal	Average	Extensive	
Shetland Sheepdog		●				●	
Miniature Schnauzer		●				●	
Beagle			●	●			●
Pembroke Welsh Corgi		●			●		
Boston Terrier	●			●			
Cocker Spaniel (English & American)			●			●	●
Staffordshire Bull Terrier	●			●			
Whippet			●	●			
Australian Cattle Dog			●		●		
Brittany			●		●		●
Basset Hound		●			●		●
Keeshond		●				●	
Bulldog	●			●			
Siberian Husky			●		●		
Samoyed		●				●	
English Springer Spaniel			●		●		●
Standard Poodle		●				●	
Elkhound/Norwegian Elkhound		●			●		
Afghan Hound			●			●	
Airedale Terrier		●					●

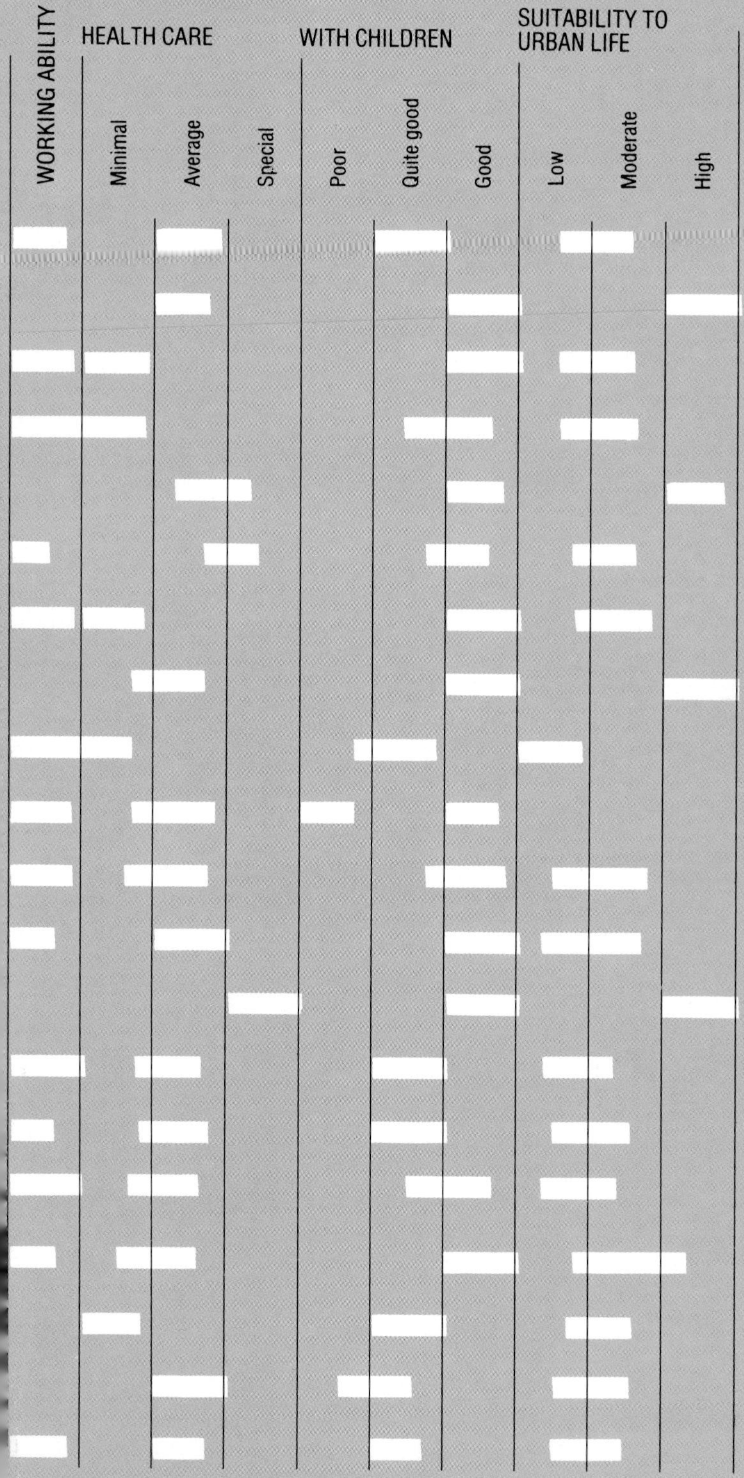
WORKING ABILITY
HEALTH CARE
Minimal
Average
Special
WITH CHILDREN
Poor
Quite good
Good
SUITABILITY TO URBAN LIFE
Low
Moderate
High

BREED	EXERCISE			GROOMING			HUNTING ABILITY
	Minimal	Average	Extensive	Minimal	Average	Extensive	
Dobermann/Dobermann Pinscher		■		■			
Bearded Collie		■				■	
German Short-haired Pointer			■	■			■
Rough Collie		■				■	
English, Irish & Gordon Setters		■			■		
German Shepherd Dog			■		■		
Dalmatian			■	■			
Weimaraner			■	■			■
Boxer		■		■			
Chow Chow		■				■	
Golden Retriever		■			■		
Labrador Retriever			■		■		
Japanese Akita/Akita		■			■		
Rottweiler		■		■			
Old English Sheepdog			■			■	
Pyrenean Mountain Dog/Great Pyrenees			■			■	
Mastiff		■			■		
Great Dane			■				■
St Bernard		■				■	
Newfoundland			■			■	

WORKING ABILITY	HEALTH CARE			WITH CHILDREN			SUITABILITY TO URBAN LIFE		
	Minimal	Average	Special	Poor	Quite good	Good	Low	Moderate	High
■	■	■		■				■	
■		■				■		■	
■		■				■	■		
■			■			■		■	
		■				■		■	
■		■			■			■	
						■		■	
■		■		■				■	
■						■		■	
	■			■					■
■			■			■		■	
■		■				■		■	
■		■			■			■	
■								■	
■		■			■			■	
			■			■		■	
	■			■			■		
		■				■		■	
		■			■			■	
■		■				■		■	

CHIHUAHA

The Chihuahua is the world's smallest dog and takes its name from a state in Mexico. Colourful legends link the forebears of the modern Chihuahua with the Aztecs, Toltecs, the Maya tribes, and with Cortes and his armies from Spain, but there is little, if any, sound information beyond the fact that the breed seems to have originated in South America. Chihuahuas need to be selected carefully, since it is not easy to breed soundness in very small size. It is preferable to see the parents and the conditions under which the puppies were reared when possible. Many Chihuahuas are spoiled by over-cossetting, and others are ruined by too much confinement. The Chihuahua is capable of being a real dog, if it is brought up sensibly from puppyhood.

Size

Height about 12.5cm (5 inches); weight between 0.9-1.8kg (2-4 lbs); the largest, which make the most acceptable pets, up to 2.7kg (6 lbs).

Colours

Any colour permissible in any combination.

Coat Varieties

Smooth coated – soft, close-fitting hair with ruff around neck. *Long coated* – soft, long hair with fringe on ears and feathering on legs and tail.

Grooming

Smooth coated – minimal, except for brushing with soft, natural bristle brush and rubdown with silk cloth. *Long coated* – brushing with small pin brush, followed by thorough, gentle combing.

Life Span

Can be very longlived, up to 18 years.

Health Problems

Vulnerable to fractures and other accidents in puppyhood. Some of the breed have a *molera*, an unclosed section of the skull which can remain open throughout life; this makes the dog prone to injury and should be avoided.

Plus Points

Very intelligent and easy to train, can be kept entirely indoors if absolutely necessary, using a litter box like a cat, so tiny they can be easily carried and can rest on an invalid's bed without causing a problem, very comforting to their owner and the smooth coats are said to be suitable, even therapeutic, to asthmatic children, and those allergic to dog hair, exercise needs moderate.

Minus Points

Fragile, decidedly suspicious to people except owner. Caesarian birth is common, dislikes cold, not naturally a mixer with other dogs or people, can be too fragile and nervous for mixed-age families.

Ideal Home

A "lap" dog, it responds well to comfort and companionship without over-pampering. Ideal pet for solitary individuals or elderly, as well as invalids, wheelchair-bound people, and others who have difficulty in walking, but are living in their own home.

Smooth-coated Chihuahua

POMERANIAN

The Pomeranian is a member of the Spitz group of sled and herding dogs from the North, and in most recent history came from Pomerania in Germany. The breed has steadily been diminished in size, from the working dog of about 13.6kg (30 lb) in weight, to the 6.3kg (14 lb) type, popular in the 19th century, down to the show Pom of today which weighs in at about 1.8kg (4 lbs). In miniaturization, some soundness of the original has been lost. The breed, usually white in the mid-18th century was quickly taken up by fashionable ladies and Gainsborough included many in his paintings. Today, the tiny Pomeranian is very much a show dog, as the profuse coat which is such a feature of the breed requires so much care.

Size
Height about 17.5cm (7 inches); weight up to 3.1kg (7 lbs), 1.8-2.2kg (4-5 lbs) show dogs.

Colours
Many solid colours, bright orange-red being most popular.

Grooming
Up to 30 minutes daily brushing so that coat stands away from the body giving the admired "ball of fluff" appearance.

Life Span
About 12 years.

Health Problems
Possible early tooth loss; weak, discharging eyes and tear staining; dislocation of knee joint.

Plus Points
Portable size, devoted to owner, very well suited to apartment life (can be paper-trained), adaptable about exercise, equally enjoying walks with owner or exercise in limited space, good alarm dog.

Minus Points
Can be short-tempered and noisy, not particularly good with children, profuse coat shedding in summer.

Ideal Home
With mature, possibly elderly or sedentary individuals in city or town apartment who cannot give the dog regular outdoor exercise but who can devote time to the daily grooming that the Pomeranian needs.

YORKSHIRE TERRIER

This tiny, lively terrier is one of the world's most popular breeds, particularly suitable for town life today. The Yorkie, as we know it, is only about 100 years old and even so its ancestors were much larger dogs. Yorkshire weavers and coal miners created this working terrier from several different types of ratting and rabbiting dogs and also introduced the blood of the Maltese Terrier brought by sailors from the Mediterranean. The exaggerated long coat is a later development. The pet Yorkie, which can be slightly heavier than the show dog, may have its heavy coat clipped down to 7.5-10cm (3-4 inches) all over. Breeding from very tiny bitches is hazardous, as it is not uncommon for one or more pups to throw back to large ancestors making natural birth impossible. Immense popularity has led amateurs to breed these dogs so maximum care should be taken in buying. Ask for a larger specimen as a pet.

Size
Height 15-17.5cm (6-7 inches); weight about 3.2kg (7 lbs); docked tail.

Colours
Bright tan on head, lower legs, eyebrows and chest, overlaid with long, straight, steel-blue hair on body; puppies do not grow adult coat until 8-12 months.

Grooming
Clipped Yorkie needs daily combing and brushing; topknot is usually tied back with ribbon; full show coat needs hours of grooming.

Life Span
About 11 years.

Health Problems
Relatively healthy; falls or knocks can cause fractures of fragile bones; prone to bronchitis and early tooth decay; poor tolerance of anaesthetic; delicate digestion, exotic treats should be avoided.

Plus Points
Active, playful, affectionate, good alarm dog, easily trained, suits city and apartment life, needs little exercise.

Minus Points
Can be noisy and disobedient, can be belligerent with other pets, too fragile for young family.

Ideal Home
City apartment or small town house with mature owners able and willing to devote time to the dog's grooming needs; with owners who will appreciate this small, lively and responsive lapdog but not spoil it.

MALTESE

One of the oldest of toy breeds, the Maltese has a history which goes back to the Greek and Roman Empires. In Britain, in Elizabethan times and later, it was a popular lapdog with Court ladies. Maltese have no working instincts at all and behave rather like toy spaniels. They love comfort and hate cold and wet. They are easy to spoil but respond well to play and activity.

Size
Height up to 25cm (10 inches); weight between 1.8-2.7kg (3-6 lbs).

Colour
White, with long flowing hair; for show purposes, held by twin ribbon bows on the forehead.

Grooming
More than 30 minutes per day in full coat, and a bath once a week; give special attention to the area around the eyes which can become tear-stained; face should be cleaned after every meal; coat may be clipped down if kept only as a pet.

Life Span
Up to 15 years.

Health Problems
Upset digestion, chills, and discomfort in hot weather; should be paper-trained to avoid going out in extremes of weather.

Plus Points
Sensitive, gentle, loving pet, playful, moderate exercise needs.

Minus Points
May try to assume some of the attributes of a spoiled child and can be jealous of visitors, can be difficult to feed with a weak digestion, coat demands careful, daily grooming.

Ideal Home
Suits elderly or solitary people living in small town apartments or houses, which are warm and comfortable, with available time to spend on grooming the dog. Suitable for invalids or people confined to wheelchairs since indoor activity will supply sufficient exercise.

BICHON FRISE

The Bichon represents the ideal pet for many people, filling a need for a small-sized, attractive and companionable dog. From the Mediterranean region, this charming dog was particularly popular with the French and Spanish nobility in the 18th century, after which it generally declined in favour until fairly recent times. Breeding has only taken place in earnest over the last 15 years and in both Britain and North America, this hitherto little-known dog is rapidly gaining in popularity. Would-be owners should go to a reputable breeder of this dog since once popularity increases, so also does indiscriminate breeding which can lead to multi-hereditary defects and unsoundness in the animal.

Size
Height up to 30cm (12 inches); weight between 3.2-5.4kg (7-12 lbs).

Colours
Pure white, but cream, grey or apricot hairs are permitted.

Grooming
Demanding, 20 minutes brushing each day to retain the full fluffy appearance.

Life Span
Quite long, up to 15 years.

Health Problems
Few; regular brushing of the coat, and skin massage will protect against skin problems; feed three times a day to counteract a tendency to low blood-sugar exhaustion.

Plus Points
Attractive Poodle-like appearance, happy, intelligent, very good with children, excellent, easy-going pet, which needs little exercise.

Minus Points
Fastidious grooming is necessary and requires frequent and expensive professional trimming.

Ideal Home
Well suited to city life in apartment or small house where one family member has time for daily grooming.

| # MINIATURE PINSCHER

One of the fascinations of this ancient breed is the way the dog moves, lifting its front feet high in the manner of a hackney pony. The Min Pin, as it is familiarly known, is brave beyond its size, quick and clever and apt to think it is stronger and more powerful than its owners. This trait can make the Min Pin a difficult dog to own despite its small size. Although this toy dog looks like a model of a Doberman Pinscher and many behave as if they were Dobermans, the breeds are not related. The Min Pin has a long history, at one time the pampered lap dog of German nobility and later a champion performer in the rat pit. The breed found favour in America before it was taken up in Britain, but now its popularity is increasing all over the world as a suitable breed for adults living in small accommodation. The tendency to guard food and toys to unreasonable extent, and the quick snapping jaws make the dog unsuitable for tiny children, and special care should be taken when children come to visit. The Min Pin can be very fond of the children in its own family, provided it has been taught its rightful place from puppyhood. This is a dog which cannot take any indulgence and its treatment must be kind but firm. The Min Pin will find enough exercise in a medium-sized garden and it is capable of keeping itself amused provided the garden is well fenced and has no holes where it can squeeze out. However, the breed cannot stand the cold and should never be left without access to a warm house.

Size
Height 25-30cm (10-12 inches); weight about 4.5kg (10 lbs).

Colour
Black with tan, solid reddish tan, chocolate with tan, or grey/blue, docked tail.

Grooming
Regular brushing and rub-down.

Life Span
Up to 12 years.

Health Problems
Generally hardy, except for possible dislocation of joints; dislikes cold.

Plus Points
Minimal grooming, good watch and alert dog, an indoor dog which need not be taken out in cold and wet weather, portable.

Minus Points
Can be dominant, snappy, and very noisy, restless, and constantly busy around house and garden, feels the cold excessively.

Ideal Home
With adults, in small warm house or apartment with medium-sized garden, who will not indulge the dog or allow it too much of its own way.

PEKINGESE

This little dog was kept in secret for many centuries in the palaces of China and known to the Western world only in paintings or embroidery. They were never sold and only given to foreigners as a great mark of favour; and these rarely survived life outside the Imperial court. In the course of the Anglo-Chinese War of 1858, five Pekingese (two pairs plus an extra bitch) were taken by British commanders and brought to England. One was presented to Queen Victoria who called the dog "Looty", showing true Victorian candour about the origins of this prize. In England, the dogs became known as 'Pekingese' after the city in which they were first found. The breed became a status symbol in Edwardian England and was considered a dog of the aristocracy. It has been one of the most popular toy dogs in Britain and North America since the early years of this century. The Peke is relatively hardy and need not be a lapdog. It is courageous, and clever and quite sporting in its own way.

Size
Height about 20-22.5cm (8-9 inches); weight about 4.5kg (10 lbs) UK, not over 6.3kg (14 lbs) US.
Tiny pekes, known as 'sleeves', may be born in any litter but they are rare and perhaps not so hardy.

Colour
Almost any solid colour, and parti-colours with white.

Grooming
Brush and comb every day, no trimming, wash face and bathe eyes.

Life Span
To 15 years if sensibly reared and given a good balanced diet.

Health Problems
The prominent eyes can be a problem (may be irritated by grass seeds or dust, and a fall or a fight may cause the eye to fall out of the socket); breathing difficulties in hot weather.

Plus Points
Beautiful, loyal but not demonstrative, ornamental, good housedog, independent.

Minus Points
Obstinate, self-willed, may be difficult to feed and given to refusing to eat as much to show dominance over its owner as to lack of appetite, not suitable for small children.

Ideal Home
With quiet or mature adult owners who will provide the home comforts Pekes like, as well as occasional exercise and games. A restful pet for people who work at home and well suited to town or city life.

Related breeds
Tibetan Spaniel, a hardier little dog with less exaggerated facial features than the Peke. Tibetan Spaniels are tipped to be one of the popular breeds of the future.

MINIATURE DACHSHUND

Dachshunds occur in two sizes, Standard and Miniature, and in three coat types, smooth, long-haired and wire-haired, so they offer a particularly wide choice of type within one breed. While the Miniatures are lighter in weight than some toy dogs, all Dachshunds are classified as hounds, and they retain a hound's scenting power and quality of endurance. The modern Dachshund originated in Germany, being bred with powerful body and short legs in order to penetrate badger setts. *Dachs* is German for badger, but its other German name, *Teckel* (short) reflects its diminutive height. The Germans also bred into the Dachshund a voice which is loud and penetrating for a dog of its size. The continuing bark was needed so that hunters could locate the dog while it was underground. The breed also has the qualities of endurance and persistence, which when used in hunting is a virtue, but may be annoying in a pet which will not stop a particular behaviour pattern. The breed has undergone several swings in popularity. Due to antipathy to all things German in World War I, Dachshunds were scorned and even stoned in the streets and it was not until after World War II that the breed was truly acclaimed by the public again. It is still a favourite in Europe, America and Britain.

In the US, the AKC recognizes one breed with three varieties and the two sizes are judged against each other. In the UK, six separate breeds are recognized and the winners only compete together in the group finals where they also compete with all other hounds.

Size
Height about 12.5cm (5 inches); weight under 5kg (11 lbs), US under 4.5 kg (10 lbs) at 1 year old. *Standard:* height about 22.5cm (9 inches); weight from 4.5-9kg (10-20 lbs).
Many permitted, both solid colours and dappled.

Grooming
Long-haired requires daily combing and brushing; *wire-haired* needs professional trimming twice a year; *smooth-haired* requires regular rubdown with damp cloth.

Life Span
12-14 years.

Health Problems
Obesity; spinal problems (disc disease leading to paralysis is not uncommon); inherited eye disease leading to loss of sight in mini longhairs; skin troubles in smooths; where available, insurance for veterinary fees advised.

Plus Points
Sporting, active, intelligent, playful; smooth-coated variety requires minimal grooming.

Minus Points
Persistent barking, compulsive digging, obstinacy, refusal to be handled, can be irritable and very quick to bite, jealous and inclined to fight other dogs.

Ideal Home
With adults plus adolescent children in small town or country house with walled garden in which dog can run. With owners who enjoy having an active dog but are prepared to be firm with the dog from puppyhood, and to give the dog short frequent walks.

Related breeds
Dachsbracke, a rare German hunting dog, larger and heavier than the Standard Dachshund with a thick, Corgi-type coat. It is a very rare breed nowadays.

Smooth-haired Dachshund

Wire-haired Dachshund

Long-haired Dachshund

CAVALIER KING CHARLES SPANIEL

The ancestor of this appealing breed, one of which is the house pet of the US president, and of its smaller, short-nosed and less robust cousin, the King Charles Spaniel, was the English Toy Spaniel. A favourite with the English monarchy for 300 years since the time of Charles II (who is shown in paintings by Van Dyck with these dogs), this breed developed over the last century into the two distinct varieties recognized in Britain today. The smaller, short-nosed variety, the King Charles Spaniel, is known in the US as the English Toy Spaniel and shares with the Cavalier the same four colourings and easy-going temperament. In order to protect the Cavalier variety from exploitation, the fancy in the US has not sought AKC recognition, although the Cavalier Club has its own registration system and around 500 puppies are bred each year with many also imported from the UK.

King Charles Spaniel

Size
Height 20.5-33.7cm (10-13½ inches); weight 8-9kg (18-20 lbs).

Colour
Tricolour (black/white and tan), black with tan markings, ruby (chestnut red with no markings), Blenheim (chestnut and white).

Grooming
Daily brushing of coat essential.

Life Span
12-14 years.

Health Problems
Generally hardy but keep ears clean and healthy and wipe tear stains from eyes, dislikes cold and wet conditions; buy with care, preferably from a reputable breeder.

Plus Points
Attractive appearance, good-natured, good with children, other dogs and people, minimal exercise needs, well-suited to urban life.

Minus Points
Not particularly intelligent, can be too gregarious, may bark unnecessarily, needs regular grooming.

Ideal Home
With single individuals or easy-going families in apartment, small town or country house who want an agreeable companion dog which is not too demanding.

BORDER TERRIER

The Border, the tough little terrier from Northumberland and Cumberland on the Scottish border, lives to work and lovers of the breed are keen that these attributes should not be lost. Its instincts are to chase and kill quarry, and traditionally Borders work closely with foxhounds. They will also hunt vermin along river banks and around farmyards with the greatest enthusiasm. Their work makes these dogs strongwilled, self assertive and determined, but they have great respect and affection for a firm owner. They are good dogs about the house, and are even-tempered and pleasant with children and other dogs.

Size
Height about 30-32cm (12-13 inches); weight about 5.4-6.8kg (12-15 lbs).

Colours
Shades of red, blue or tan.

Grooming
Regular stripping and tidying of coat.

Life Span
Up to 14 years.

Health Problems
Generally healthy, except for need to keep the coat free of fleas and ticks which may cause skin irritation; flea collars should not be worn while working.

Plus Points
Energetic, keen vermin exterminator, reliable, trainable, intelligent, hardy, excellent with horses, fine companion for country children, needs little grooming.

Minus Points
Needs active, working existence, not suitable as an idle pet, not well suited to city or suburban life, rare breed in US.

Ideal Home
In country, ideally on a farm where there is sufficient exercise for this unspoilt, active dog.

Related breeds
Norfolk Terrier (drop-eared) and *Norwich Terrier* (prick-eared), both excellent companion and sporting terriers, which make splendid, cheap-to-maintain pets for those who admire a terrier's bustling energy.

CAIRN TERRIER

The Cairn Terrier takes its name from the cairns, or heaps of stones, peculiar to Highland Scotland from which the dogs were used to bolt otters and fox which had gone to ground. Like all terriers, these dogs snap habitually (although not from a vicious tendency) and their manner makes them unsuitable around very small children.

Size
Height about 25cm (10 inches); weight about 7.2kg (16 lbs), in US 5.8-6.3kg (13-14 lbs).

Colours
Red, sandy to brindle, and grey to nearly black. The coat changes a great deal in colour between puppyhood and maturity.

Grooming
10 minutes twice a week, with professional handstripping of the puppy coat at about five months old, twice yearly handstripping thereafter.

Life Span
Up to 17 years.

Health Problems
Very few, apart from food allergies and skin problems. Litters may be large for the size of dog.

Plus Points
Hardy, energetic, independent, easily trained, an amusing dog, lively and alert, entertaining to watch and walk with, good with older children and an excellent family companion which will be content in most environments.

Minus Points
Children under five years need to be supervised with puppies, inclined to fight with other male dogs, prone to dig in the garden and may burrow under sheds and fences.

Related breeds
Scottish Terriers (see page 54), *West Highland White Terriers* (see page 52) and *Skye Terriers*, all hardy little terriers from the Highlands of Scotland where they were at one time interbred.

| # LHASA APSO

The Lhasa Apso, one of four breeds indigenous to Tibet, has a romantic background, since the monks of the Tibetan monasteries believed that when they died, their souls would enter the body of one of these little dogs. It is uncertain whether their name originated from the Tibetan name *Abso Seng Kye*, or "Little Bark Dog", or from the Tibetan word *rapso*, meaning "goat". These dogs with thick coats against the cold were believed to stand on the ramparts of the monasteries in the mountains and to bark a warning when strangers appeared. The breed in America was started by a direct gift of dogs from the Dalai Lama.

Size
Height about 25cm (10 inches); weight about 6.3kg (14 lbs).

Colours
Any permissible.

Grooming
Very demanding, thorough brush every day and grooming weekly.

Life Span
About 10-14 years.

Health Problems
Generally a very healthy dog; skin problems if the coat is not kept free of parasites.

Plus Points
Good watchdog with loud persistent bark which gives the impression to intruders of a much bigger dog, exercise needs moderate, keeps busy around house and garden, attractive when well kept, affectionate with owners, suitable for town life.

Minus Points
Suspicious of strangers, will not welcome friends or allow them to touch it, can be noisy, may be too nervous around children, especially visiting children, can be strong-willed, inclined to fight if other dogs are kept, needs lots of grooming.

Ideal Home
Small apartment or house in town or country with relatively solitary owners who have time for daily grooming and who will make this strong-minded little dog the centre of their lives. Suitable for the elderly and also excellent hearing dogs for the deaf. Not ideally suited to young children.

Related breeds
Shih Tzu (see page 50) and *Tibetan Spaniel*, both pretty dogs with slightly Oriental faces. Both make agreeable companion animals but some are inclined to noisy barking and they are not very responsive to admirers outside the family.

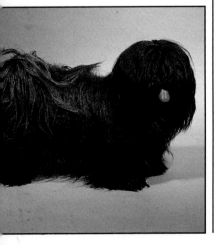

PUG

This is a cheerful, amusing, clean little dog which will gladden the heart of many an owner. It makes a delightful family pet and will be willing to assume a child-like role if that is what the owner wants. Believed to be one of the most ancient of dog types, Pugs were the pets of Buddhist monks. They were introduced to Britain by the Dutch House of Orange and these little dogs soon took over as court favourites from the toy spaniels favoured by the Stuart monarchs. Perhaps the most famous Pug in history is the Empress Josephine's "Fortune" which bit Napoleon on their wedding night.

Size
Height about 25-30cm (10-12 inches); weight between 6.3-8kg (14-18 lbs).

Colours
Black, silver or fawn with black "trace" line from top of head to the tightly curled tail.

Grooming
Daily brush and cleaning of the facial wrinkles.

Life Span
12-15 years.

Health Problems
Respiratory troubles in hot weather, bad ventilation and with vigorous exercise, not the easiest whelpers.

Plus Points
Small size, clean coat, low maintenance costs, loves to be cossetted but will also enjoy a romp, adjusts well to apartment and city life.

Minus Points
In older age will snore and wheeze, can be jealous of visitors and will tyrannize owners if allowed to do so.

Ideal Home
Town family with children, business person who can take the dog to shop or office, elderly people who will enjoy giving it short walks, people who want a small dog which is more responsive than the Peke or Tibetan breeds.

SHIH TZU

This very old breed, whose name is Chinese for "lion" is also known more picturesquely as the "Chrysanthemum-faced dog", from the unique hair growth radiating from a centre point above the stop. Probably of Tibetan origin, these little dogs were, like the Pekingese, highly prized in the Chinese Imperial court and it was not until the early years of this century that they were imported into Europe. Controlled interbreeding with Pekingese, under the supervision of the Kennel Club (England) for four generations, during the 1950s, helped establish the Shih Tzu as we know it today. This breed is now a very popular pet and show dog in Britain and America, where its introduction was mainly due to dogs brought home by servicemen returning after World War II.

Size
Height about 25cm (10 inches); preferred weight not below 4kg (9 lbs) and not over 7.2kg (16 lbs).

Colours
All colours, black noses except in liver-coloured dogs.

Grooming
In full flowing show coat, the Shih Tzu should be brushed daily and have its whiskers washed after each meal; and it should have a shampoo and blow dry once a week. Pets very often have the coat clipped to 5cm (2 inches) long all over and this can look extremely attractive, as well as being practical; show dogs usually have hair fastened on top of the head to prevent it falling over the eyes.

Life Span
10-12 years; does not age visibly.

Health Problems
Few; teeth need regular veterinary attention as they tend to be lost early; spinal disc disease caused by a long back and short legs may be a problem.

Plus points
Sweet natured, aristocratic bearing, quiet in the house, dependent on human companionship and a distinctive pet, needs minimal exercise.

Minus Points
Not very clever, passive, sometimes touch-shy, obstinate, needs daily grooming.

Ideal Home
This breed is equally at home in town or country houses and apartments where owner is prepared to spend time on grooming and giving the dog human companionship. Although show dogs are generally kept indoors, this breed loves outdoor walks and really enjoys snow. The Shih Tzu gets on well with children when encouraged to play and not handled too roughly.

WEST HIGHLAND WHITE TERRIER

Like the Cairn Terrier, this dog was a working terrier hunting fox and badger. It can still hunt small vermin very efficiently but is now an extremely popular companion dog because of its attractive white coat, lively disposition and manageable size. Like all terriers, it is inclined to snatch or make other quick movements which may startle or be misinterpreted. It is therefore not an ideal dog for very small children, but as a companion for older children or adults it can hardly be bettered. A very stylish breed, more trimmed than the Cairn, it still retains all the sporting instincts of its race.

Size
Height about 28cm (11 inches); weight about 7.7-8.6kg (17-19 lbs).

Colours
Pure white only, black nose, dark eyes.

Grooming
Twice weekly brush, hand-stripping twice per year; keep coat clean by brushing rather than shampooing, as bathing tends to soften the crisp hair.

Life Span
About 12-14 years.

Health Problems
Generally healthy except for possible chronic skin problems; where available, insurance for veterinary fees advised.

Plus Points
Attractive appearance, outgoing personality, good with children, good watchdog, eager to learn.

Minus Points
Can be noisy, needs extensive grooming.

Ideal Home
Suitable for town or country family with time for grooming, exercise and constructive play that this small dog likes.

JACK RUSSELL TERRIER

There must be thousands of owners, at least in the UK, who believe they own a Jack Russell, although these dogs are a dissimilar lot with great variation in size and shape. It is for this reason that the British Kennel Club has, as yet, been unable to accept it as a breed. Breeding a distinctive type of terrier was a hobby of English country gentlemen in the 1880s and particularly of sporting parsons like the Rev. John Russell of South Devon. From boyhood he was interested in hounds, hunting and especially in the small terriers which were put down to bolt a fox which had gone to ground. Eventually he came by what he described as the perfect terrier, game and keen, small in size, white with a tan patch over each eye and ear, and with a short wiry coat. The Rev. Russell bred from this bitch and kept a register of pedigrees, but it is believed that the demand for his terriers was such that he also bought in and resold puppies. Probably the Jack Russell never was a pure bred strain but that then, as now, any small terrier, white in colour with hound markings could qualify for the name. In Britain, it has become very popular in recent years as a household pet.

Size
Height about 35cm (14 inches); weight about 6.3kg (14 lbs).

Colours
White with hound markings.

Grooming
Minimal, except for regular stiff brushing.

Life Span
About 15 years.

Health Problems
Not easy to pinpoint as breeding is not organized or standardized, but Jack Russells are known to suffer from deformity of knee and hip joints, staggering gait and eye diseases.

Plus Points
Sporty, lively companion, manageable size, minimal grooming needs.

Minus Points
Not yet a recognized breed, can be short-tempered.

Ideal Home
With hunting or sporting family who will provide plenty of activity or work for this energetic, lovable little dog.

SCOTTISH TERRIER

While stemming from the same ancestry as the Cairn and Westie, the Scottish Terrier, known familiarly as the Scottie, is more dour than its relatives. It can be reserved in adulthood even with its owners and tends to be suspicious of visitors to the home. It keeps busy and active both indoors and out. The Scottish Terrier is probably more suitable as a companion to older children, although many individuals get on well with children under five – often becoming their protectors. This breed is not for everyone, but it does have a large, loyal following of devoted enthusiasts.

Size
Height about 22.5cm (9 inches) at the shoulder; weight about 9.5kg (21 lbs).

Colours
Harsh, dense coat may be various shades of brindle, black, iron or steel grey, sandy or wheaten.

Grooming
Twice weekly brushing, professional handstripping advised twice yearly.

Life Span
10-14 years.

Health Problems
Skin diseases, allergies, difficult whelping.

Plus Points
Hardy, independent, courageous, a good house dog which adapts well to city or town life.

Minus Points
Not effusive or demonstrably affectionate, noisy and very reserved except to owners, difficult whelpers, handstripping is necessary and expensive to maintain harsh coat, may kill other small animals, including cats.

Ideal Home
With town or country dwellers, who will give the dog the regular exercise and long walks it needs. The breed has independence developed to a high degree and is best suited to people who consider this temperament a plus factor.

This dog is similar in many ways to the Rough Collie, although half its size. They have a common ancestry, but the Sheltie is not a miniature of the Rough Collie. Like all the animals from the islands of the far North, Shelties are diminutive, but they are very clever and effective working dogs for use with sheep and goats. They are now also very popular as pets and they make excellent if somewhat noisy housedogs.

Size
Height about 35cm (14 inches), in US between 32.5-40cm (13-16 inches); weight about 9kg (20 lbs).

Colours
Sable and white, tricolour, and blue merle.

Grooming
Needs regular brushing; this breed also sheds heavily in autumn and spring.

Life Span
12-14 years.

Health Problems
Like the Rough Collie, there is a tendency towards inherited malformation and disease of the eyes; can also be affected by displacement of the patella (kneecap), which is thought to be inherited.

Plus Points
Handy size, charming expression, good alarm dog, excellent family dog which adapts well to town or city life.

Minus Points
Some poorly bred Shelties are very shy and will not allow themselves to be touched by strangers; noisy persistent barking.

Ideal Home
With mixed-age family living in suburbs or country, fond of grooming, able to spend time on constructive play and long walks with the dog every day.

Related breeds
Rough Collie and *Smooth Collie* (see page 88).

| # MINIATURE SCHNAUZER

The dog is a small replica of the Standard Schnauzer. The breed has a long history, dating back to the 15th and 16th centuries in Europe, originally bred as a guard or stable dog. The Miniature excels as a rat catcher, and in Germany ratting trials are held in order to keep the working ability in the breed which is now so popular as a companion dog. The Miniature Schnauzer is shown in the Terrier Group in US and the breed does indeed have many terrier characteristics, but in Britain they join the Utility Group. The Standard and Giant Schnauzers share most of the characteristics of the Miniature Schnauzer. Because of its size, however, the Giant Schnauzer is best suited to country life.

It is used as a police dog in Germany, takes obedience training well but can be aggressive towards other dogs.

Size

Height 30-35cm (12-14 inches); weight about 6.8kg (15 lbs). *Standard:* height 46-48cm (18-19 inches); weight 18-22.5kg (40-50 lbs). *Giant:* height 65-70cm (25½-27½ inches), dogs, 60-65cm (23½-25½ inches) bitches; weight 34-58.5kg (75-95 lbs). Shape should be almost square; in the US, the Miniature Schnauzer has cropped ears.

Colours

Mixed colour coat of light and darker banded hairs with white whiskers, eyebrows, cheeks, legs and feet, known as pepper-and-salt, black, or black and silver.

Grooming

The coat is harsh and wiry over a soft undercoat; twice a year hand stripping is necessary to preserve the smart outline; the long hair on the muzzle, which is distinctive of the breed and known as the "beard" should be washed daily, but the dog should not be bathed all over as this softens the coat; light daily grooming with a wire glove keeps the skin healthy and removes dead hair.

Life Span

Longlived, up to 15 years, showing no signs of age until quite late in life.

Health Problems

Few, this is a healthy breed; tendency to hereditary eye problems, and eyes of breeding stock should be checked for this.

Plus Points

Very intelligent, quick and lively, easy to train, smart appearance when correctly trimmed, enjoys participating in family activities, good with children, good alarm dog around house and garden, adaptable to city or country life.

Minus Points

Can be noisy, overprotective of possessions, snappy if not taught manners early in life, not immediately friendly to visitors, not a dog for elderly or sedentary people.

Ideal Home

In city, town or country in mixed-age family with children with whom it can enjoy romps, good walks and occasional off the leash runs. From puppy days, the dog should be regarded as a minor child, required to behave properly but allowed to participate in family activities and adventures.

Giant and Miniature Schnauzer

Standard Schnauzer

BEAGLE

The Beagle is probably the oldest of the scent hounds and for hundreds of years has been kept in packs to hunt hare. It is only in the last 30 years that Beagles have been kept as individual pets by people with no intention of hunting. While the dog has many endearing qualities, the over-riding instinct to leave home territory at every opportunity in order to follow scent has made pet ownership of the Beagle something of a problem. Generally they should be exercised on a leash or in an enclosed space, so helping to control their wanderlust. The dog should always wear a collar and identity tag, in case it gets lost.

Size
Height to 40cm (16 inches) UK, standard to 37.5cm (15 inches) US, small under 32.5cm (13 inches); weight, standard about 9kg (20 lbs).

Colours
Any hound colour or marking.

Life Span
15 years or more.

Health Problems
The Beagle experiences few health problems and is generally fit and active throughout its life.

Plus Points
Easy to feed, excellent temperament with children, adults and other pets; gentle and affectionate, submissive to owners, needs little grooming.

Minus Points
Strong tendency to wander, prone to howling especially in confinement, hunting pack Beagles should never be bought or accepted as pets since they will be impossible to housetrain and will have a strongly-developed hunting instinct.

Ideal Home
The Beagle is equally suited to a large or small house, preferably with walled garden, good gates and noise-tolerant neighbours. Although they can keep themselves fit in a small garden, owners should enjoy walking with the dog regularly on a long, extending lead.

PEMBROKE WELSH CORGI

The Pembroke Welsh Corgi is a working cattle dog and was hardly seen outside of the Welsh Principality until the 1920s. It is best known for its association with the British Royal Family. Her Majesty Queen Elizabeth II has had pets of this breed since her childhood. The Pembroke Corgi may trace its ancestry to the Spitz breeds of Northern Europe. It appears to have different roots from the Cardigan Corgi, which is said to be related to the Dachshund, although the two Corgis have some similarities in appearance. The Corgi's traditional work is to round up and drive cattle by snapping at their heels, and a very good job it does, too. As a pet, this instinct must be discouraged by training the dog from puppyhood to be a reliable companion dog.

Size
Height 30cm (12 inches); weight about 10kg (22 lbs), a size which can be lifted and carried, if necessary. Docked tail.

Colours
Fawn to glowing red, tricolour or black and tan.

Grooming
Not difficult, thorough brush twice a week.

Life Span
Up to 15 years.

Health Problems
Very few, except for the possibility of spinal disc disease progressing to paralysis of the hind limbs.

Plus Points
Clever, quick and lively, a good companion on walks of any length, easy to groom and keep clean, a pleasing outline, size and colour, hardy, good alarm dog and good family dog.

Minus Points
Can be very noisy, given to prolonged barking, can be snappy if not controlled.

Ideal Home
Practically anywhere, from a smallish apartment to a large country house, provided plenty of companionship is given to the dog and it is not left alone for long periods. A lot of exercise is necessary and on farm land the dog is liable to round up livestock unless controlled. Many owners have pairs of Pembroke Corgis.

Related breeds
Cardigan Corgi, which does not have docked tail; *Lancashire Heeler*, an easy-to-keep, hard-working pet although its appearance is not striking; and *Swedish Vallhund*, a bright and alert cattle herding dog, higher on the leg than Corgis.

Cardigan Corgi

BOSTON TERRIER

The Boston Terrier is the ideal dog for many would-be pet owners. It is intelligent, active enough to be interesting, smooth-coated and pleasant to handle, long-lived and handsome. An extremely affectionate dog with its owners, it is also genial with friends and even casual acquaintances. Its grooming needs are minimal and it needs regular, but no lengthy, exercise. However, the Boston Terrier is difficult to breed. The massive rounded head makes natural delivery by smaller bitches virtually impossible, so that elective caesarians are the custom in many kennels. This makes the Boston Terrier an expensive puppy to buy although there are self-whelping lines to be found, probably from larger bitches. It is worthwhile seeking out such a strain as the naturally whelped puppy is likely to be stronger and more protected against disease in infancy. An American breed, the Boston Terrier's ancestors include the English Bulldog and the Staffordshire Bull Terrier. However, the modern Boston has no terrier characteristic and no fighting instinct, nor is it classed as a terrier at any kennel club. The modern Boston is perhaps closest in appearance to the French Bulldog. Whatever the ancestry, this national American dog approaches the ideal in exclusive housepets and would be even more popular if the bitches did not have such whelping problems.

Size
Height about 40cm (16 inches); lightweight up to 6.8kg (15 lbs), heavyweight up to 11.3kg (25 lbs).

Colours
Brindle or seal and white is the favoured colouring, with the white markings evenly distributed on head, chest and legs; patched puppies are less desirable; in US this breed has cropped ears.

Grooming
Minimal; a polish with a silk cloth on dark areas smartens up the coat. The white areas keep sparkling clean if the dog is in good health.

Life Span
Up to 17 years.

Health Problems
Prominent eyes are subject to injury and some strains have a tendency to demodectic mange (these bitches should not be bred from); where available insurance for veterinary fees is a wise precaution.

Plus Points
Clever, clean, handy size, good playmate for children, gentle but responsive to friendly overtures, alert housedog but never bites, always civil to guests.

Minus Points
Expensive, difficult to breed because of whelping problems, mischievous as puppies, snores loudly in middle to old age.

Ideal Home
The Boston Terrier is adaptable to most home environments, whether in city, town or country and will live happily with solitary individuals or families who enjoy walking it and playing simple games with it.

The Boston Terrier was first known as the American Bull Terrier. It was given full recognition in 1893 as the Boston Terrier, in honour of the city responsible for its development.

COCKER SPANIEL (ENGLISH)

The English and American Cocker Spaniels are different in appearance although they stem from the same ancestry. The American Cocker is smaller and has a longer coat than its English cousin. Both breeds are excellent hunters, although the American Cocker is well adapted to city life. Both breeds are immensely popular worldwide as companion dogs because of their merry lively temperament.

Size
Height about 40.5cm (16 inches); weight about 13.6kg (30 lbs); docked tail.

Colours
A very wide variety of solid colours and parti-colours.

Grooming
Daily brushing and combing to prevent matting of coat.

Life Span
One of the longest lived, up to 16 years.

Health Problems
Ears need constant care and cleaning; inherited eye disease and kidney troubles; woolly overgrowth of coat in spayed bitches; tendency to overweight; where available, insurance for veterinary fees advised.

Plus Points
Merry temperament, cheerful, energetic and willing, excellent gundog, good with children and other dogs.

Minus Points
Enormous popularity and over-breeding has brought about some serious temperament faults in some cockers of red and golden colouring and some blacks. Needs regular exercise, daily grooming necessary.

Ideal Home
Home in suburbs or country, where large garden gives opportunity for exercise. Owners should be keen walkers, possibly able to keep two cockers together.

AMERICAN COCKER SPANIEL

Size
Height about 38cm (15 inches); weight about 12.4kg (28 lbs).

Colours
As for English Cocker Spaniel.

Grooming
Long coat needs thorough brushing and combing daily, plus professional trimming every 8-10 weeks.

Life Span
As for English Cocker Spaniel.

Health Problems
As for English Cocker Spaniel.

Plus Points
Excellent family pet, easy going, affectionate, easily trained and obedient.

Minus Points
As for English Cocker Spaniel; daily grooming and brushing particularly important, plus professional trimming every 8-10 weeks.

Ideal Home
Companionable city or country home preferably with garden where dog can be active and not overindulged. Owners should be prepared to give dog sufficient and regular exercise.

| # STAFFORDSHIRE BULL TERRIER

The Staffordshire loves a fight and will quite often pick a quarrel with other dogs just for the sake of it. Yet this is a lap-sitting breed within its own home, wonderful with children, and almost never attacks people. Originally known as a Bull and Terrier, its ancestors of the 1800s were the older, more athletic type of Bulldog and probably the larger Black and Tan Terrier of those times. The infusion of terrier blood has produced a more independent dog than the Bull breed tends to be, while retaining devotion to its family, a welcoming approach to visitors, and a strong guard and attack attitude to wrongdoers. The Staffordshire finds a lot of amusement in a big garden, hunting and killing vermin, and also devising for itself pastimes which increase its fighting ability, such as swinging on a rope. The Staffordshire is always in training for its next contest and it can bring its owner a lot of trouble if not strongly supervised and managed.

Size
Height to 40cm (16 inches), weight about 16.3kg (36 lbs); *American Staffordshire Terrier* – height to 47.5cm (19 inches),

American Staffordshire Terrier

weight about 22.6kg (50 lbs) for males. This larger dog has cropped ears and is not recognized in Britain.

Colours
Almost any colour, plain or with white, except black and tan.

Grooming
Minimal – quick rub with a hound glove and polish of coat with silk cloth once per week.

Life Span
10-12 years.

Health Problems
Generally healthy, hardy breed; owners should watch for signs of discomfort or injury as with all fighting breeds; breeding stock should be screened for hereditary cataract; where available, comprehensive insurance including veterinary fees and third-party cover is advisable.

Plus Points
Good-natured, amusing, extremely loyal family pet, good with children, excellent guard dog.

Minus Points
Liable to fight other dogs, can be aggressive with strangers, needs firm discipline as a puppy, difficult to exercise in urban areas, even on the lead.

Ideal Home
With mixed-age family in average to large country house with securely fenced garden. Adult owner should be able to take dog on regular, supervised, long walks, occasionally allowing dog to swim or play in water.

Related breeds
Bull Terrier and *Miniature Bull Terrier*. Smooth-coated, in attractive marking and colours, the *Bull Terriers* are devoted to their owners, interesting to own but can be a problem because of their tendency to fight and kill vermin. Not for the novice owner who wants a quiet life.

WHIPPET

As a pet in the home, the Whippet is pure pleasure with a gentle, good-natured temperament and graceful appearance. Outside is another matter. The Whippet is one of the fastest of all dogs and impossible for a human runner to catch at an average of 56km (35 miles) per hour. If, therefore, you want to own a Whippet, you must be sure of safe, enclosed exercising ground and a high degree of obedience training. Many breed clubs organize informal racing for Whippets.

Size

Height 46.2cm (18½ inches) dogs UK, 47.5-55cm (19-22 inches) dogs US; 43.7cm (17½ inches) bitches UK, 45-52.5cm (18-21 inches) bitches US; weight 12.7kg (28 lbs) males, 9kg (20 lbs) bitches.

Colours

Any.

Grooming

Minimal. Occasional rubdown with damp cloth. Very little coat shedding.

Life Span

About 15 years.

Health Problems

Needs protection against cold (wearing a coat is advised in winter). Prone to stomach upsets and skin problems.

Plus Points

Affectionate and gentle with all ages, graceful, elegant appearance, a restful dog indoors.

Minus Points

Exercise very important, will pursue and kill cats and other small animals, if given the opportunity.

Ideal Home

In town (provided plenty of exercise on the lead is given) or country, preferably where it can be exercised away from traffic. The breed thrives if kept in pairs indoors where the dogs can keep each other warm.

Related breeds

Greyhound, an ancient coursing dog of which the Whippet is a recently developed, half-sized version. The show Greyhound is heavier than those bred for racing and neither are particularly easy to own, as they require so much exercise and are difficult with smaller dogs and cats. Ex-racing Greyhounds can make good pets since they are used to wearing muzzles at exercise but will need intensive housetraining if they have always been kennelled; *Italian Greyhound*, the smallest of the Greyhound family, weighing only about 3.6kg (8 lbs) and 32.5cm (13 inches) high. With all the fine-boned elegance of the rest of the family, the Italian is a relatively fragile dog but can make a wonderful pet for adults. It is prone to leg fractures and is a high risk for anaesthetics.

AUSTRALIAN CATTLE DOG

The Australian Cattle Dog and its smaller relative, the Kelpie, are essentially working dogs. They are able to endure harsh conditions and to cover many miles in a day when herding sheep and cattle over vast distances. These two dogs were bred from imported collies from Scotland, with the addition of Dalmatian and Dingo blood as well as some admixture of other breeds. The result is a superlative working dog, agile in mind and body and able to sum up a situation quickly and think for itself. They come into their own on the huge sheep and cattle stations of Australia where their talents are used to the full. Although they can make fine companion dogs if properly socialized from puppyhood, they are not suited to town life. These tireless, willing and clever animals will not be fully occupied unless given some work or a great deal of exercise and will not be content as simply a household pet.

Size
Height about 50cm (20 inches); weight about 15.8-18kg (35-40 lbs).

Colours
Red or blue speckled.

Grooming
A stiff brush once weekly; remove mud from the coat; keep free of parasites, particularly sheep ticks.

Life Span
About 12 years.

Health Problems
Few known, only the best survive in working conditions. Inherited deafness can be a problem.

Plus Points
Hardy, loyal, protective of owner and family, good watchdog.

Minus Points
Not friendly with visitors or other dogs, requires a great deal of exercise, not good with children except for family members it has known since puppyhood.

Ideal Home
With strong dominant owner in the country, preferably farmer or agricultural worker who is able to use dog's special talents.

Kelpie

BRITTANY

The Brittany is a gundog par excellence, taking its name from the province of France where it is thought to have originated. Although this breed was not imported into the US until the 1930s, it is now an American favourite. By comparison, it is somewhat rare in Britain. The Brittany is a willing worker, with a very keen nose, and excellent hunting ability in a very conveniently sized dog. It loves very rough shooting, going through thickets and bramble with no hesitation at all, and it points game like a setter so that it does not flush them out before the guns are within range.

Size
Height 47.5cm (19 inches); weight to 20kg (44 lbs) UK, 18kg (41 lbs) US.

Colours
Orange and white or liver and white.

Grooming
Brushing twice a week, removal of mud and thorough drying after hunting.

Life Span
About 12 years.

Health Problems
Ears must be kept clean, free of parasites and infection; arthritis in old age.

Plus Points
Excellent working dog, loyal, affectionate, intelligent, very sensitive to correction, easy to train.

Minus Points
Unsuitable as a non-working dog, miserable in idleness, noisy and destructive if confined, bored or left alone.

Ideal Home
With farming or hunting owner where dog will get plenty of exercise in open country working as a partner with owner, not really suited to city life.

BASSET HOUND

It is generally agreed that the Basset Hound is an obstinate dog, often with a mind of its own, especially in pursuit of quarry. It is, however, a superbly good-tempered breed and lots of fun to own. The Basset comes from France and was developed from Bloodhound stock – hence its wonderful capacity for following scent, if rather slowly and deliberately. This dog will never excel at obedience work (it may be easier to fetch your Basset than to call it) and is not clever. It is a lovable dog but not particularly easy to own.

Size
Height to 37.5cm (15 inches) UK, 35cm (14 inches) US; weight about 20.4kg (45 lbs) UK, up to 27.2kg (60 lbs) US.

Colours
All hound colours acceptable.

Grooming
Minimal; occasional rubbing and polishing of coat; and removal of mud or dirt.

Life Span
Up to 11 years.

Health Problems
Bloat is a post-feeding hazard which regular exercise helps to prevent (dog should be kept observed for several hours after feeding); possible lameness and eventual paralysis because of short legs and heavy, long body.

Plus Points
Good natured, excellent with children, more cheerful than its appearance suggests, deep musical bark.

Minus Points
Strong hound instincts, especially in following a scent, can be disobedient when following quarry, "doggy" smell; needs exercise three times daily to avoid obesity.

Ideal Home
Family house in town or country with largish ground floor area (Basset has difficulty climbing stairs) and adequately fenced or walled garden to prevent dog from following quarry; access to safe exercising ground essential; owners must have a sense of humour and be able to devote time to caring for this dog which does not like being left alone.

Related breeds
Petit Basset Griffon Vendéen, a small, rough-coated hunting dog from France which is gaining popularity as an amiable pet and a good, warning house dog.

The Keeshond is another member of the Northern Spitz group, but in modern times it is usually associated with the trading barges of the Rhine and the canals of Holland. Many of the bargees kept one or two of these hardy dogs on their boats, and it is said that the Kees's ability to curl up into a small ball and make itself unobtrusive comes from an ancestry of living in close quarters. Once on land, the Keeshond is a great walker and has adapted well to urban life. The breed tends to be something of a one-man dog, taking little notice of anyone but close family members. It is not very responsive to visitors.

Size
Height up to 45cm (18 inches); weight about 18.1kg (40 lbs).

Colours
Abundant long-haired topcoat grey with black tips, thick cream undercoat.

Grooming
Daily brushing plus 45 minutes thorough grooming weekly; if desired, seek professional advice on how coat should be groomed for maximum attraction.

Life Span
Up to 14 years.

Health Problems
Generally hardy; does not thrive in hot, humid conditions.

Plus Points
Glamorous appearance, good watchdog, lives easily with other animals, fine companion dog.

Minus Points
Can be noisy, dislikes heat, requires considerable grooming, profuse coat shedding in spring.

Ideal Home
With town or country owners keen on long walks, which this dog needs, and willing to devote time to grooming.

Related breeds
Norwegian Elkhound (see page 80), *Finnish Spitz* and *Pomeranian* (see page 34) are all members of the Spitz group, characterized by full coats and bushy tails carried curled over the back. All are energetic, inclined to be noisy and require a lot of grooming.

BULLDOG

For 600 years from medieval times, the Bulldog was used exclusively for baiting (teasing and fighting) tethered bulls. Baiting just before the bulls were slaughtered was said to make the meat more tender, but the practice soon became a popular spectator sport. The shortened face was a useful attribute, allowing the dog to get a grip on the bull's nose as it lowered its head to charge. A courageous dog would hang on, even when swung high in the air by the bull, and often would be badly injured. All the "Bull" breeds retain the ability to ignore pain, especially while fighting. Bull baiting in Britain was forbidden by law in 1835 and thereafter the Bulldog's fighting ability was bred out and its physique modified. The modern Bulldog, with its many physical incapacities, is the direct result of man's "improvement" of the breed. Today, the Bulldog is a docile creature, despite its appearance, which gives and should receive total devotion from its owner.

Size
Height about 37.5cm (15 inches); weight 22.6-25kg (50-55 lbs) UK, 18.1-22.6kg (40-50 lbs) US.

Colours
Any, except black/white, black or black/tan.

Grooming
Minimal. Occasional brushing and rubdown of coat; facial folds should be cleaned and dried twice daily.

Life Span
Short, up to 7 years.

Health Problems
Breathing problems, poor eyesight, susceptible to heat stroke in warm weather or hot rooms and cars; puppies often delivered by caesarian section because of broad head.

Plus Points

Amusing, loyal, clean, courageous, good with children, excellent guard dog, requires little exercise after reaching maturity, well suited to apartment life.

Minus Points

Needs constant vigilance and attention, especially in warm weather, becomes quickly distressed in cars or when travelling, snores loudly, tires easily with exercise, expensive to buy because of difficult births and health hazards.

Ideal Home

In town or city house or apartment (*not* walk-up, Bulldogs dislike stairs) with family or mature/elderly people who will give this dog the care and affection it needs.

French Bulldog and *Boston Terrier* (see page 60). Both are expensive to buy because of whelping problems but they make clever and attractive companions, fond of good living and, being smooth-coated, they are clean to handle.

| # SIBERIAN HUSKY

The Siberian Husky was bred and developed as a lightweight sled dog by nomadic tribes in north-east Asia. Huskies first appeared in America during the Alaskan Gold Rush of the 1900s when Husky teams displayed their legendary qualities of speed, coordination and endurance to survive in the hardest conditions known to man. They also proved to be more equable in temperament than the Malamutes previously used. The Alaskan Malamute, a related breed, is a very powerful load puller and pack carrier but not as fast in a sled as the Husky. Siberian Huskies achieved worldwide fame in 1925 when a team of 20 dogs, led by the male Togo saved innumerable lives by rushing vital anti-diphtheria serum over 218km (350 miles) to the isolated city of Nome, Alaska. The exhilarating sport of Husky team racing has grown rapidly in the US, and in Scandinavia and Switzerland but is still in its infancy in Scotland and England. Husky puppies look like teddy bears and are almost irresistible. However, think carefully before you buy, as the Husky will not have a happy life as an idle pet.

Size
Height about 55-57.5cm (22-23 inches); weight about 22.6-27.2kg (50-60lbs).
Colours
Any colour.
Grooming
Twice weekly brushing; twice daily during heavy coat shedding in spring.
Life Span
12-14 years.
Health Problems
Generally healthy; possible hereditary eye disease; breeding stock should be screened and certified.
Plus Points
Charming equable temperament, good with children, clean.

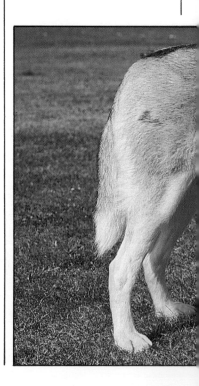

Malamute

Minus Points

Can be neurotic and destructive if kept confined or inactive, howls when unhappy, tendency to wander if allowed unsupervised freedom, heavy coat shedding in spring, no guarding instinct.

Ideal Home

As one of a pair or team of Huskies in country home with active family, preferably engaged in winter sports or who want to train the dogs to harness and take part in trailing. The dogs should live in unheated, secure quarters with walled or fenced yard but be given constant human companionship.

SAMOYED

Devotees of these beautiful dogs call them the "Smiling Sams". When greeting its owner or visitors, the Samoyed's gentle expression, kind eyes and great good humour exude a warm welcome. The Samoyed takes its name from a tribe which lived a nomadic existence north of the Arctic Circle. The dogs were used to guard herds of reindeer, but shared the life of their masters, eating and sleeping with the family in their tents. Thus they came to regard all human kind as their friends, an attribute which the Samoyed has brought into Western life. This breed was introduced to Britain in 1894 and is now a popular breed in both the UK and US.

Size
Height up to 57.5cm (23 inches); weight up to 34kg (75 lbs).

Colours
White, possibly with small biscuit-coloured markings.

Grooming
Daily brushing; keep clear of fleas and ticks; heavy coat shedding in summer.

Life Span
Up to 14 years.

Health Problems
Generally hardy, except for tendency to inherited heart disease.

Plus Points
Beautiful appearance, friendly to guests yet good guard dog, adores human company.

Minus Points
Needs daily vigorous exercise, can be destructive if left alone too often, heavy shedding of top and undercoat once a year, needs cool climate.

Ideal Home
With mixed family in country or town house with large walled or fenced garden where dog can exercise; owners must have time and inclination to take dog on long walks and hikes, to play games in the snow (which this breed loves) and to give it the constant human companionship it needs.

ENGLISH SPRINGER SPANIEL

As the name suggests, the English Springer Spaniel was originally used for flushing out or "springing" game for the hunter's net or to be killed by hounds or falcons. These handsome dogs are the forebears of all working spaniel breeds, except the Clumber. There is some difference between the working strains, which compete at field trials by showing their working ability, and show strains which are often larger and heavier with a better-preserved coat. If you require one with inherent working ability, it is best to seek out one of the working strains.

Size
Height about 50cm (20 inches); weight about 22.6kg (50 lbs); docked tail.

Colours
Various, usually liver or black with white markings.

Grooming
For companion dogs, daily grooming with professional trimming twice yearly; for working dogs, washing or brushing off of mud and thorough drying following a shooting expedition; ears must be kept clean and dry.

Life Span
12-14 years.

Health Problems
Possible eye diseases; haemophilia in some lines; ear infection, arthritis in old age; choose only healthy animals.

Plus Points
Loyal, affectionate, good with children, mixes well with unfamiliar people and animals, a fine companion dog, eager and active working dog, good alarm (but not guard) dog, adapts to town and city life.

Minus Points
Needs work and/or hard exercise, loves water and may be constantly wet and muddy, giving off "doggy" odour.

Ideal Home
Family home in country with farming and/or rough shooting activities; equally well suited to home or city life if not too confined and given vigorous exercise plus occasional trips to countryside (if not trained to the gun, keep your Springer under control on game preserves or it will pursue quarry).

Related breeds
Welsh Springer, a smaller dog with glowing red and white coat. A tireless worker, born to live in the country, very good with children and not aggressive with other dogs.

STANDARD POODLE

The fun-loving Poodle will share a wide range of activities with its owner from duck shooting and wildfowling to dancing and circus tricks. It also enjoys being dressed up and shown off as a fashion accessory. In fact, the Poodle is an adaptable dog and quick to learn, as long as its cleverness is utilized and it feels the centre of admiration. For more than 200 years Poodles have been the favourite dog of circus and cabaret acts, due to the dog's ability to stand and perform dancing movements while on the hind legs. Poodles delight in learning tricks and in imitating their owners, but this is a sensitive breed which must not be bullied or roughly handled. This fine dog should only be purchased from the most reputable breeders.

Size
Height over 37.5cm (15 inches), weight about 23.5kg (52 lbs). *Miniature:* height 27.5-37.5cm (11-15 inches) UK, 25-37.5cm (10-15 inches US), weight about 7kg (15½ lbs). *Toy:* height under 27.5cm (11 inches) UK, under 25cm (10 inches) US, weight about 2.7kg (6 lbs); docked tail.

Colours
Wide range of solid colours from white through apricot to silver and black; puppies with white splashes on solid colours make excellent pets but are unacceptable in the show ring.

Grooming
Six-weekly professional trimming and bathing for both "lamb" clip and "lion" clip (essential for show dogs); no hair shedding.

Life Span
Up to 16 years.

Health Problems
Possible skin rash from unskilled use of clippers or allergy to shampoo and/or colour reinforcer; in miniature and toy varieties, possible heart disease, eye conditions and joint malformations.

Plus Points
Highly intelligent with sense of humour, lively watchdog, generally friendly to strangers, decorative.

Minus Points
The poodle's great popularity has led to some poorly bred dogs which are acutely sensitive, excitable and nervous, needs constant attention and expensive maintenance, toy vulnerable to rough handling, accidents and hereditary diseases.

Ideal Home
Suited to small, average or large dwelling with individuals or family who appreciate an intelligent and beautiful dog and who will give the dog varied exercise, play and human companionship.

Miniature Poodle with lamb clip

Toy Poodle with lion clip

ELKHOUND/NORWEGIAN ELKHOUND

This Scandinavian hunting dog can trace its ancestry back to the time of the Vikings when it was used to track and pull down bears and wolves, and the elk (moose). Elkhounds made themselves useful in many other ways, acting as guards to sheep and homesteads, and pulling sledges. Elsewhere, the Elkhound will track fox, raccoon, lynx and even mountain lion. In Scotland Elkhounds have been used to track wounded deer in the forests, and they are also handy around a farmyard, killing rats, mice and rabbits. A latter day role for this versatile dog is with mountain rescue teams, tracking climbers stranded on the peaks; it has also scented out victims of major disasters buried under rubble.

Size
Height about 51.2cm (20½ inches); weight (males) about 25kg (55 lbs).

Colours
Mixed shades of grey.

Grooming
Daily brush and comb; extensive shedding of top and undercoat.

Life Span
Up to 16 years.

Health Problems
Generally healthy; hip dysplasia, some eye problems; breeding stock should be checked and certified.

Plus Points
Loyal, good with children, useful guard.

Minus Points
Needs plenty of work or exercise plus firm discipline in puppyhood, shrill bark, can become destructive and self-mutilating if kept confined in urban surroundings, needs cool conditions.

Ideal Home
In country home or on farm with owner engaged in outdoor work where dog can be employed as a working partner; or in town or suburbs with owner whose hobby is participating in canine sport activities such as obedience training, tracking, sledding or agility trials.

AIREDALE TERRIER

The Airedale, the largest of the terriers is nicknamed the "King" of Terriers and was bred specifically for otter hunting along the banks of the River Aire in Yorkshire. The Airedale is too large to follow its quarry to ground, but speed, courage and great strength make it an excellent hunter of small and big game in water or on land. This powerful dog was also developed as a guard and messenger and in the early part of this century was used to police docks and railways and in World War I by the British and Russian armies and the Red Cross. It has also done well as a utility gundog. Like all terriers, the Airedale can be quick to snap, and may resent being touched by strangers. As the breed is capable of reaching a high level of obedience training, this should be started early and maintained firmly, otherwise the dog can become a liability to its owner.

Size
Height 57.5cm (23 inches); weight about 22.6kg (50 lbs); docked tail.

Colours
Harsh wiry top coat in black and tan, or grizzle and tan; oily waterproof undercoat.

Grooming
Daily brush and comb; twice yearly handstripping to preserve the typical outline.

Life Span
To 14 years.

Health Problems
Little to note other than tendency to skin rashes, especially if clippers are used instead of handstripping.

Plus Points
Smart, good size, loyal protective family dog with a wide variety of talents, very hardy.

Minus Points
Can be quick tempered, may kill small domestic animals, including cats, if the opportunity presents itself.

Ideal Home
With family in country or suburban house; this breed must have brisk walks and lots of physical activity every day, needs to be handled firmly from puppyhood.

Related breeds
Otter Hound, a large web-footed dog, eminently fitted to hunt vermin along river banks. Otter Hound packs are now kept to hunt mink which have escaped from captivity and which do much damage to wildlife. This breed is not really suitable as a house pet.

AFGHAN HOUND

The Afghan Hound reached a peak of popularity in the 1960s, the Flower Power era, when this proud, aristocratic hunting dog was bought mainly as a fashion accessory by people who understood little about the breed's nature or requirements. The Afghan is not an easy dog to keep and is by no means an ideal dog for urban dwellers. This fast-running desert hound is difficult to exercise off the lead and can be deaf to all entreaties when it takes off after game. Long walks on a lead are therefore a necessity. A somewhat fey, aloof dog, the Afghan will not respond warmly to visitors although it can be amusing and affectionate within the family. Above all, this breed needs time for grooming, exercise and obedience training and only a relatively small number of people have sufficient time to serve this large, beautiful dog properly.

Size
Height about 67.5cm (27 inches); weight about 22.6kg (50 lbs).
Colours
All colours.
Grooming
Daily brushing of long coat (up to an hour) to prevent tangles from forming; many wear snoods indoors to protect ears from food bowls.
Life Span
Up to 14 years.
Health Problems
Generally healthy; breed has a low pain threshold, thereby "suffering" even with minor injuries; breeding stock should be screened for inherited cataract.

Plus Points
Dignified, beautiful appearance, devoted to and affectionate with family and children.
Minus Points
Obstinate, sometimes disobedient, if poorly trained can be shy, sensitive and nervous, needs lots of exercise, can be suspicious of strangers.
Ideal Home
In large country house with garden where owner can devote time to grooming, exercise and obedience training that this breed needs; in town or city apartment, owner must be able to take dog on long brisk walks several times a day.
Related breeds
Saluki, a beautiful hound of ancient lineage which comes from the Middle East where it was used to course gazelle. Elegant and sensitive, the Saluki is not for the rough and tumbles of family life and is not a dog which takes to obedience easily. Safe exercising ground is essential for this breed since the Saluki runs very fast and is not always trustworthy with other animals; *Sloughi*, a rare African sight hound which looks similar to a smooth-haired Saluki but is heavier in body; *Borzoi*, a Russian coursing dog, is a gentle biddable pet within the home but something of a problem when exercising and outside the home. The speed at which this tall dog can move and its determination to catch and kill other small animals can make the graceful Borzoi a difficult breed for all but the specialist owner.

DOBERMANN/DOBERMAN PINSCHER

Familiarly known as the Dobe, this guard dog is a lasting tribute to the skill of a German dog breeder and tax collector, Louis Dobermann, who developed this breed in the 1880s. His personal need was for an alert, energetic, fearless and loyal guard, and he was successful in creating just such a dog, although the earliest examples were not as refined and elegant as the Dobermanns of today. The exact ancestry of the Dobermann is not known but the bloodlines certainly contain Rottweiler, the old German Pinscher, Black and Tan Terrier, Pointer and Greyhound. The resultant dog was first recognized in Germany in 1900, and is now used by police and armies the world over. Prospective owners should be used to dogs and must realize the responsibility they undertake in owning a dog which can, at worst, be a killer. Handling must be sensitive, kind but firm and the Dobermann must be given sufficient exercise to avoid irritability and tension.

Size
Height to 67.5cm (27 inches) dogs, to 62.5cm (25 inches) bitches; weight 31.7kg-34kg (70-75 lbs) dogs, 27.2-29.5kg (60-65 lbs) bitches; tails docked, ears cropped except in UK.

Colours
Black with tan markings, red/tan, blue/tan and fawn or Isabella colouring.

Grooming
Minimal, regular rub down with rough cloth.

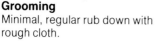

Life Span
About 12 years.

Health Problems
Generally healthy; possible cervical spondylitis (wobbler syndrome) due to fusion of neck vertebrae and compression of spinal cord; possible inherited blood disorder (Von Willebrands disease); obesity in middle age; veterinary check advisable before purchasing puppy.

Plus Points
Extremely high standard of obedience if patiently trained when young, highly intelligent, very loyal to owners, perfect guard dog, clean, minimal grooming.

Minus Points
Can be too sharp in defence, aggressive to callers, extremely reserved with people outside immediate family, would not suit a convivial owner.

Ideal Home
With serious owners, preferably in country house with some land, who have time to train dog from puppyhood. Dobermanns must have an authoritative master and need plenty of exercise or work.

| # BEARDED COLLIE

This is one of the oldest farm dogs and was probably originally used for driving cattle across the Highland roads of Scotland on the way to market. It is an ideal companion dog for a family, provided it is given regular grooming and the right kind of exercise. It dislikes a confined existence and is more suited to country life than town or city life.

Size
Height to 55cm (22 inches); weight to 25kg (55 lbs).

Colours
Many shades of grey, brown, sandy or black with or without white markings.

Grooming
Daily brushing to keep coat in good condition; little hair is shed.

Life Span
About 12 years.

Health Problems
Generally healthy; dense coat may conceal external parasite infestation.

Plus Points
Good tempered, affectionate, easy to train, intelligent and good with children.

Minus Points
Needs daily hard exercise and grooming, natural herder of people and animals, noisy barker but not a watchdog.

Ideal Home
Mixed-age family home, preferably in country or adjoining open land where dog can take off the lead runs and plenty of exercise; excellent farm dog and in windy, rugged or wet areas, since the dog will go out in all weathers.

GERMAN SHORT-HAIRED POINTER

There is said to be a Pointer, Foxhound and probably Bloodhound in this breed which evolved in the late 19th century. The result is a smart, clean limbed, all-purpose hunting dog which will find, point, mark the field and retrieve on land or from water for all types of game. The breed has become deservedly popular in the US and Britain as both a working dog and a show dog. It is almost unfair to keep this working dog as an urban pet, since close confinement can turn such a dog into a neurotic casualty.

Size
Height to 62.5cm (25 inches); weight about 31.7kg (70lbs).

Colours
Solid liver, or liver/white ticked, spotted or roan.

Grooming
Minimal; brushing once or twice per week and removal of mud.

Life Span
About 12 years.

Health Problems
Generally healthy; possible hip dysplasia; entropion (ingrowing eyelashes); arthritis in older age.

Plus Points
Clever, hardy, willing, good-tempered, performs well at all hunting tasks, good with other dogs and children.

Minus Points
Hyperactive if not adequately employed, unsuited to urban life.

Ideal Home
With farmers or hunters who will give dog the vigorous exercise it needs in open spaces and in water.

Related breeds
Wire-haired Pointer, developed in the late 19th century in Germany as an all-purpose hunting dog from interbreeding Pointer, Poodle, hounds and terriers. An outdoor dog which must have work to be happy.

ROUGH COLLIE

The beautiful Rough Collie, once known as the Scotch Collie, and beloved by generations of children as the *Lassie* of films and stories, is now in a sorry state. Continuing popularity over many years and poor breeding has led to several inherited eye diseases which can lead to defective sight. Over 80 per cent of the breed in America are said to be affected, and 65 per cent in Britain. Collies are also subject to hip dysplasia. It is therefore essential to buy Collies only from the most reputable breeders. The Collie is an ancient breed, a working sheepherding dog which probably came to Scotland with invaders from Northern climates. Queen Victoria did a lot to popularize the breed both in Britain and the US. Many of the early Scottish settlers in America brought their Collies with them as working dogs, but when two Collies from the Queen's Balmoral kennels were imported, the breed was taken up by the rich and fashionable and has remained at the top of the popularity list ever since. Few modern Rough Collies work with sheep anymore but it should not be forgotten that they are outdoor dogs and they need a lot of exercise and free running both in bad weather and in fine, but not as much grooming as might be imagined. A variety of the Collie breed is the Smooth Collie, of the same stature as the Rough but with a hard, dense, smooth coat. This variety is traditionally associated with cattle droving and has never been as popular a pet as the Rough Collie.

Size
Height about 62.5cm (25 inches) UK, 57.5cm (23 inches) US; weight about 27.2kg (61 lbs) UK, 22.7kg (50 lbs) US.

Colours
Sable and white, tricolour, blue merle and (in US) white.

Grooming
Brushing twice weekly for approximately one hour; coat does not generally tangle or matt except on spayed bitches which grow an excess of woolly hair.

Life Span
14-16 years.

Health Problems
Generally healthy although prone to eye defects and hip problems leading to acute lameness and arthritis; veterinary clearance certificate for these diseases are advisable before purchasing a puppy.

Plus Points
Extremely gentle, affectionate companion for children, obedient and kind, attractive and graceful appearance, good watch dog.

Minus Points
Shrill, prolonged bark, profuse shedding of top and undercoat in spring and autumn, plenty of free exercise required.

Ideal Home
With companionable and devoted family in largish house or apartment where there is access to garden or open space so that the dog can get regular and extensive outdoor activity.

Rough Collie with Shetland Sheepdog

Smooth Collie

ENGLISH, IRISH (RED) AND GORDON SETTER

The three breeds of Setter, English, Irish and Gordon (a Scottish breed), were all used as gundogs in Britain and elsewhere until fairly recent times when their role has been largely taken over by all-purpose breeds. The Irish Setter is also known as the Red Setter. A two-coloured variety, the Red and White is found in the UK and Europe but is unacceptable in the US. The English and Irish Setters are particularly elegant and graceful dogs and can be wonderful family pets for country dwellers.

Size
English and Irish (including variety *Red and White*) – height 62.5-67.5cm (25-27 inches); weight 27.2-31.7kg (60-70 lbs). *Gordon* – height 62-66cm (24½-26 inches); weight 25.4-29.5kg (56-65 lbs).

Colours
English – white with orange or lemon ticking, roan (red ticking), blue belton (black ticking) with similar patches on head and ears; puppies born white with ticking development later. *Irish* – mahogany or chestnut red (*Red and White* – white with red patches). *Gordon* – black with typical tan markings.

Grooming
Coat of English and Irish Setters should be well-combed and brushed daily to maintain beautiful appearance. Gordon requires moderate coat care with regular brushing.

Life Span
9-12 years.

Health Problems
Hip dysplasia (male and female breeding stock should be officially evaluated); eye diseases in Irish Setter (annual examination advised); skin problems, especially on feet in English Setter.

Plus Points
Graceful, beautiful dogs, kind and patient with children, respond to teaching, trustful temperament.

Minus Points
Boisterous, awkward and frustrated in small spaces, need human company as well as abundant exercise, can reach high shelves and scent what is hidden, no guarding instinct.

Ideal Home
With companionable family in large country house where owners are fond of walking and outdoor pursuits and can give dog plenty of exercise. Owners should be patient and consistent in behaviour, setting standards of discipline from puppyhood. Setters love human company and playing with children.

Gordon Setter

English Setter

Irish Setters

GERMAN SHEPHERD DOG

This dog has given unlimited service to man as a working dog with police and armed forces worldwide, as a guide dog for the blind, mountain rescue dog, and as a superb personal companion and guard. The German Shepherd (known as the GSD) is capable of the finest and most heroic canine behaviour, but in the wrong hands, or put into a confusing situation without sensible direction, this dog can be dangerous. Although sometimes known as Alsatian, it is more correctly called German Shepherd Dog. It is a pity that unjustified fear makes people behave unnaturally when near a GSD, as this gives a wrong impression to this very sensitive dog which then tends to be on the defensive. To own a GSD is a great responsibility, but also a great pleasure. Buy a GSD very carefully from an established breeder of companion dogs, never from stock advertised as having excessive guarding qualities.

Size

Height to 65cm (26 inches);
weight up to 40.8kg (90 lbs);
some bitches are much lighter.

Colour

Almost any colour (white is
unacceptable in the show ring).
about 50 per cent of breed are
long coated.

Grooming

Coat sheds considerable hair so
thorough daily brushing is
essential.

Life Span

Up to 13 years.

Health Problems

Indiscriminate breeding has led
to hereditary diseases such as
hip dysplasia, blood disorders,
digestive problems (probably of
nervous origin); epilepsy and
dwarfism; unusually small

puppies should never be
purchased since such small
dwarfs are short-lived.

Plus Points

Impressive physique and
appearance, great loyalty to
owners, quick intelligence and
learning ability, trainable to a
high degree of obedience, barks
only when necessary.

Minus Points

Requires constant
companionship of owner for
exercise, constructive play and
grooming; vigorous exercise
(brisk walks on a lead for 4-5
miles per day) essential for this
active dog capable of great
endurance; owner must be
constantly aware that dog can
misinterpret innocent actions of
other people; German
Shepherd must be protected
from stress situations and not
left on its own.

Ideal Home

With confident owners who
enjoy training and working with
a dog and who will give
maximum consideration to the
dog. Owners must never tease
or roughly handle this breed
which should never be taught to
attack, except by professionals.
The German Shepherd is not for
nervous or insecure owners and
should never be left with people
of this nature.

Related breeds

The four Belgian shepherd dogs
— *Malinois* (fawn and black),
Lakenois (fawn rough coat),
Tervueren (red), *Groenendael*
(black) and the *Beauceron*, a
French short-haired sheep dog.
None of these sheep-herding
dogs has been as intensely bred
as the German Shepherd Dog
and so may be more suitable as
a guard/companion. The
Lakenois is the most rare
because of its unprepossessing
appearance.

DALMATIAN

Commonly known as Spotted Dick, the coach dog or the firehouse mascot dog in US, the Dalmatian takes its name from the province of Dalmatia on the Yugoslavian coast. It is an ancient breed which in its time has fulfilled many roles, but is now chiefly remembered as a breed trained to run with horse and carriage. Initially a guard dog against robbers and highwaymen, it gradually became in the 18th century a gentleman's companion and a graceful ornament to his equipage. An adaptable breed and quick to learn tricks, the Dalmatian is a frequent circus performer. It is sensitive and responsive to human companionship and becomes melancholy without it. A discreet, quiet guard dog, the Dalmatian is a little too bouncy in youth with young children. Because of its inherent capacity to run at high speed for many miles, there is a great need for sustained exercise, otherwise the dog may become frustrated and destructive.

Size
Height about 47.5-57.5cm (19-23 inches); weight about 25-29.5kg (55-65 lbs).

Colours
White with either black or liver spots; show requirements are demanding about size and distribution of spots.

Grooming
Minimal, except for occasional rubdown with hound glove and final polish; coat "wears clean" and baths are seldom needed.

Life Span
10-12 years.

Health Problems
Inherited defects can include total deafness (can be tested in six-week old puppy), urinary stones and skin allergies, especially to synthetic fibres in carpets and upholstery.

Plus Points
Good-natured, docile and kind, playful with children, smart appearance, minimal grooming, intelligent and alert, trainable to high degree of obedience.

Minus Points
Needs lots of lengthy exercise, sheds profusely twice yearly.

Ideal Home
With sports-loving owners, such as joggers, cyclists and equestrians, preferably in the country where the dog can exercise unimpeded on open ground. Town or city owners must have the time and inclination to give the dog long, vigorous runs (it should be led on roads with motor traffic).

The Dalmatian's popularity in recent years is partly the result of the Walt Disney film, A Hundred and One Dalmatians, *made in 1959 but still re-shown regularly.*

WEIMARANER

This is a German gundog, previously used for very large game such as wolves and bear. It probably has some relationship to the Pointer, and indeed was known as a Weimar Pointer when the breed was in the exclusive ownership of the Dukes of Weimar and given only to friends among the nobility. Its unique mouse-grey coat is part of the attraction of the breed. The Weimaraner differs from most gundogs in that it is not so equable with other dogs. It is also self-willed although capable of a high degree of obedience. This is not the easiest of gundogs to own, but it is a dog to be proud of when under strict control.

Size
Height to 67.5cm (27 inches); weight about 34kg (75 lbs); docked tail.

Colours
Coat any shade from mouse-grey to silver-grey; light amber, grey or blue-grey eyes, grey nose.

Grooming
Minimal, weekly brush and polish with silk cloth.

Life Span
10-12 years.

Health Problems
Generally healthy, except for tendency to epilepsy.

Plus Points
Unusual gundog with distinctive appearance, minimal grooming, good watch and guard dog, does well in obedience competitions.

Minus Points
Can be noisy, quarrelsome, destructive and unsociable, needs frequent vigorous exercise.

Ideal Home
With firm owners, preferably in country house, willing to train and control the dog. Ideally this breed should be given work either as a gundog or obedience competitor or alternatively lots of exercise in open spaces. Not a dog for casual family ownership.

BOXER

The Boxer is a relatively new breed, having been designed and developed by German enthusiasts in the late 19th century as an army dog. The Boxer's ancestors were the Bullenbeiser, the medieval bull baiting dog, and the old, tall type of English Bulldog, with the addition of other Mastiff-like descendants, giving a dog with immense courage, great tolerance to pain, loyalty and devotion to its owners, and a persistence of purpose which can be useful, but also exasperating when the purpose does not agree with its owner's ideas. Bred as a personal guard dog, the Boxer has also been used as a guide dog for the blind and in police work. This is a dog which hates to be parted from its owners, and it can be very destructive when confined away from people. Very high intelligence and an intuitive interpretation of its owner's reactions makes it a very reliable guard which seldom makes mistakes.

Size
Height about 58.5cm (23 inches); weight about 30kg (66 lbs); breed has cropped ears (US) and docked tail.

Colours
Fawn, brindle or red, with or without white markings.

Grooming
Minimal, regular brushing of coat.

Life Span
11-14 years.

Health Problems
Accident prone in youth, high incidence of cancer later in life.

Plus Points
Loyal and devoted to family, excellent playmate for children, highly intelligent and quick to learn, minimal grooming requirements.

Minus Points
Can be aggressive with other dogs, needs lots of human companionship, can be too boisterous or exuberant for frail or elderly owners.

Ideal Home
With energetic family in average to large-sized house in town or country prepared to give the dog not only regular vigorous walks and off the lead runs but also the physical and emotional contact with humans that the dog needs.

| # CHOW CHOW

This all-purpose guard and tracking dog has had a somewhat chequered career. One of the oldest breeds of dogs, it was prized in north-eastern Asia for both its flesh and its fur. Since the first of the breed came to Britain in the 1880s, to be taken up by Queen Victoria, the Princess of Wales and other titled ladies, the Chow Chow has assumed the manner of the ancient aristocracy, and perfected a technique of ignoring all except the one person it recognizes as its owner. So do not be misled by the cuddly bear appearance of Chow Chow puppies. The Chow Chow deigns to live with humans, but thinks the fewer in the household the better, and in general remains aloof, introspective and very grave.

Size
Height about 45cm (18 inches); weight about 29.5kg (65 lbs).
Colours
Any solid colour (blue/black tongue is unique to breed).
Grooming
Daily 10 minute brushing plus 30 minutes-1 hour per week with wire brush to avoid matted coat.
Life Span
Up to 15 years.

Health Problems
Generally healthy except for tendency to suffer eye irritation caused by eyelid abnormality (can be corrected by surgery).
Plus Points
Loyal guard dog, handsome dignified appearance, completely devoted to owner.
Minus Points
Essentially a one-person dog, unsuitable for busy household or children, requires fair amount of outdoor exercise so not particularly well suited to urban life, dislikes warm, stuffy conditions which can cause stress, profuse coat shedding in summer, difficult to breed.
Ideal Home
With solitary individual (although it will tolerate owner's family) in town or country house with garden and access to good walks.

Blue/black tongue, unique to this breed

| # GOLDEN RETRIEVER

Retrievers are among the most popular dogs worldwide. All have excellent scenting ability, soft mouths which can carry objects without damage, a facility for picking up articles, and a delight in presenting their owner with their "gift". Retrievers are energetic, willing workers and anxious to please, good swimmers, excellent playmates for children and are usually of very good temperament. All varieties are used as guide dogs for the blind, demonstrating their willingness to be taught. All are excellent gun dogs, and are also used as sniffer and search dogs with the police forces and armies of the world.

The Curly-Coated Retriever particularly excels in flushing and retrieving game from water. All retrievers need work or a great deal of exercise.

Size
Height about 56cm (22 inches); weight about 31.8kg (70 lbs).
Colours
Cream or gold coat (UK), gold only (US). The eventual colour of the puppy can be judged by the colour of the ears.
Grooming
Minimal, except for regular brushing.
Life Span
11-13 years.
Health Problems
Hip problems leading to arthritis in middle age; hereditary eye diseases leading to blindness; all breeding stock should undergo official screening; do not buy a puppy if this has not been done.
Plus Points
Cheerful, willing companion/ working dog, will thrive on the plainest food, good with other dogs and children, intelligent, good family pets.
Minus Points
Needs at least one hour outdoor exercise a day, and more as often as possible, needs constructive play in order to use its natural talents, doggy smell when wet, and considerable coat shedding if kept indoors, very little if any guard instinct.

Ideal Home
In average to large house, preferably in the country, with large fenced garden with active or sports loving, mixed-age family, willing to exercise the dog in all weathers. Ideal owners should want a dog to enjoy rather than fuss over.

Appearance and colours of other varieties of retriever.

Labrador Retriever
See page 102.

Flat-Coated Retriever
Black or liver coat.

Golden Retrievers

Chesapeake Bay Retriever
Straw, red or brown coat which is oily and water resistant; yellow or amber eyes.

Curly-Coated Retriever
Coat of black or liver-coloured curls which insulates the skin from wet and cold.

LABRADOR RETRIEVER

There is considerable evidence that this dog came not from Labrador but from Newfoundland and was originally one of the two types of dog from that region, the other being the large, heavy-coated dog which we know today as the Newfoundland. Also known as the St John's Water Dog, the Labrador was an invaluable mate of the North Sea fishermen. The thick waterproof undercoat, which is still a feature of the breed, enabled it to jump into icy water to retrieve fish which had escaped the nets or had jumped back into the sea from the boat. The dog would also take messages from ship to shore and would even pull in small boats. The original Labrador was an energetic and hard-working dog which thrived on the plainest and most meagre diet. Black Labradors came to Britain on fishing boats which put into the harbour at Poole in Dorset and it was not until the end of the nineteenth century that the now popular yellow dogs were introduced. Blacks are still thought to be the best working dogs, but yellows outnumber blacks in the show ring and there is currently a fashion for a deep brown colour, known as chocolate. Labradors became popular as gundogs with the decline of the expensive keepered shoots which had a variety of dogs for different purposes. Labradors make excellent general-purpose gundogs and will accomplish any task which their owner shows them how to do. They are among the most popular dogs as guide dogs for the blind and they are also used by armies and police forces to sniff out explosives, active mines, drugs and guns.

Flat-coated Retriever

Size
Height about 56cm (22 inches); weight 24.9-31.7kg (55-70 lbs).

Colours
Solid black, solid chocolate, shades of yellow from cream to bright tan (no white markings permissible).

Grooming
Minimal, regular brushing enhances coat.

Life Span
Up to 15 years.

Health Problems
Generally healthy, except for hips dysplasia (leading to arthritis in old age) and hereditary eye disease; adults should be screened and certified for both conditions.

Plus Points
Excellent temperament, good with children, equable with other dogs, learns well.

Minus Points
Watch (but not guard) dog, destructive when young, needs company and outdoor activity, constant hair shedding, "doggy" smell when wet.

Ideal Home
With mixed age active family in average to large country or town house and well-fenced garden. Owners must enjoy country walking in all weathers and constructive hide-and-retrieve games with the dog, which should be treated as one of the family.

Related breeds
Flat-Coated Retriever, an excellent worker owing quite a lot to the Newfoundland from which it was developed during the latter half of the 19th century both in the US and UK.

JAPANESE AKITA/AKITA

The Akita is a robust dog, magnificently powerful as befits an animal at one time used in its native Japan to hunt bear and deer, and later as a police and fighting dog. It will do anything its owner requires of it, endure any weather and harsh conditions, and carry out any task with intelligence and courage. Small wonder that the Akita won the admiration of American servicemen in Japan after World War II and, in due course, they brought excellent breeding stock back to their home country. It is only recently that the breed has come to Britain and Europe, but already it is gaining many devotees who are exceedingly proud of their dogs. This is a large and powerful dog which needs a dominant owner to keep it in line, otherwise it can become unruly, a danger and a nuisance to own.

Size
Height to 60cm (24 inches) UK, to 70cm (28 inches) US; weight about 49.9kg (110 lbs).
Colours
All colours with white.
Grooming
Weekly grooming of thick double coat.
Life Span
To 12 years.
Health Problems
Basically healthy except for possible hip dysplasia.
Plus Points
Strong, impressive animal, intelligent and cooperative with right owner, excellent guard or watchdog.
Minus Points
Needs firm handling (may try to dominate a weak or vacillating owner), can be aggressive with other dogs, strong hunting instinct, needs unrestrained exercise which can be difficult, dislikes warm conditions.
Ideal Home
With experienced dog owners, preferably in the country, who can maintain strict control over dog or who want to train the Akita as a hunter/retriever or guard dog. Not an easy pet or for casual owners.

Although its exact origins are obscure the Akita has been bred for over 300 years in its homeland, Akita in the northern Honshu Island in Japan.

ROTTWEILER

This is another of the descendants of the European Molossus which has retained the working ability and the intelligence which has made it a useful companion to man since the time of the Romans. The Rottweiler takes its name from the town of Rottweil in Württemberg, West Germany. During its long history it has been used for boar hunting, cattle driving and guarding but is probably best known for its role as the butcher's dog, pulling laden carts to market and returning with the money bag tied around its sturdy neck. In the 18th century it would have been a brave robber who would have tried to interfere with a Rottweiler protecting its owner's property, and this is equally true today. Although the Rottweiler has leaped forward in

Size
Height 67.5cm (27 inches) males, 62.5cm (25 inches) bitches; weight about 59kg (110 lbs) bitches.

Colours
Black with tan markings over eyes, on muzzle and cheeks, on chest and under tail which is docked.

Grooming
Minimal, regular rubdown only necessary.

Life Span
10-12 years.

Health Problems
Generally healthy, except for hip dysplasia exacerbated by over-feeding and over-exercise in youth; lameness, however temporary, should be professionally diagnosed.

Plus Points
Sober, unexcitable, quiet, intelligent, easily trainable, devoted to owner and family, formidable guard dog.

popularity in recent years both in America, where registrations have increased by 600 per cent in four years, and by 240 per cent in UK, this is not a dog to acquire casually as a burglar deterrent. There are many situations which a guard dog can misinterpret, and although the Rottweiler is of high intelligence, it also requires an intelligent owner to keep its tremendous power under control. The breed has a great deal of visual appeal, being squarish in body with sturdy legs, a short muzzle with neat ears, and a steady sagacious expression. The breed can be taught a variety of tasks which it will enjoy with its owner, including agility tests and working ability competitions, tracking and sled pulling. The self confidence which is innate to the breed makes this a difficult dog to dominate unless the owner is prepared to be always watchful and consistent in teaching good manners. The Rottweiler is not an easy dog to own properly and it can be a very dangerous dog if uncontrolled and in the wrong hands.

Minus Points

Relatively expensive to buy and rear to adulthood, resents indiscriminate advances from strangers so owner must always be vigilant.

Ideal Home

With self-assured, active owners who are serious dog owners willing to give dog exercise and work it needs. Not suited to homes with constant stream of casual callers.

| # OLD ENGLISH SHEEPDOG

This breed can trace back its history for some 150 years, so it is not particularly old. Its work, such as it is, lies more in driving cattle than herding sheep, but it is undoubtedly an English dog, originating probably in the western counties of Devon and Cornwall. The tails of this breed have always been docked or removed altogether right back to the base of the spine, thus earning the dog his nickname, the Bobtail. In recent years, the Old English has become extremely popular. As a result, working ability has been lost and the breed is kept almost entirely for its attractive appearance and massive coat. Unfortunately, new owners do not always realize the vast amount of time which must be spent on grooming to maintain the coat in its full glory and all too many Old English have been discarded in a pitiable state with infested coats. Kept in reasonable condition, the Old English is an active, jolly dog – trainable but not very quick to learn, and mischievous, bouncy and destructive when young.

Size
Height about 60cm (24 inches); weight 27.2-29.5kg (60-65 lbs); tail docked.

Colours
Grey or blue with white, especially white head. Pups are born black and white, blue shading appearing at approximately four months.

Grooming
Minimum of 30 minutes on alternate days if kept in full coat with frequent shampooing of white areas; dog should be combed right down to the skin and hair brushed from the tail forwards. For easier maintenance (not permissible in the show ring), coat can be clipped to 5cm (2 inches) all over.

Life Span
12-16 years.

Health Problems
Generally healthy; possible eye disease and hip dysplasia (veterinary check advisable before purchasing puppy).

Plus Points
Energetic, fun-loving, good with children, beautiful appearance if kept well.

Minus Points
Overbreeding has produced some animals which are slow learners, obstinate or difficult to train. Avoid any sign of bad temper in breeding stock. Coat needs constant attention. Exercise needs extensive.

Ideal Home
With mixed-age family in average to large country house with large yard. Owner must have time to devote at least two hours daily to grooming and exercise. Ideal owners should be experienced with dogs, buy with caution and take genuine pride in owning an Old English Sheepdog.

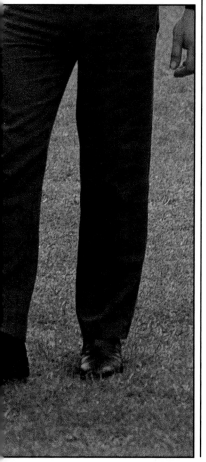

The Old English Sheepdog was first recognized as a breed in 1888. Nana in J.M. Barrie's play Peter Pan *was an Old English Sheepdog.*

PYRENEAN MOUNTAIN DOG/ GREAT PYRENEES

The work of this breed was to guard flocks of sheep against wolves and other predators, including humans, in the Pyrenean mountains of Europe. The dogs worked in pairs, surrounding the flock, and they were also companions and protectors of the shepherds, thus forming a unique canine-human bond which endures to this day. During the late 18th century the breed was popular in the French Court, and Lafayette is said to have introduced Pyreneans to America in 1828. However, it is only in recent times that this huge, mainly white, dog has been taken up as a household pet and exhibited in the show ring. An expensive dog to buy and maintain, this breed needs a lot of attention and outdoor exercise which only serious dog owners can give.

Size
Height to 70cm (28 inches) UK, to 80cm (32 inches) US; weight minimum 49.9kg (110 lbs) UK, 56.7kg (125 lbs) US.

Colour
Mainly white but badger, grey or tan markings permissible.

Grooming
Daily brushing plus more in spring when coat sheds; needs to be kept free of parasites.

Life Span
10-12 years.

Health Problems
Generally healthy, except for hip dysplasia (for which breeding stock should be screened); can develop skin problems in hot conditions.

Plus Points
Beautiful, graceful dog with strong guard ability, good with children, loyal and affectionate, good with other dogs.

Minus Points
Profuse shedding of white coat, requires lots of space and exercise, dislikes warm rooms, wary of strangers.

Ideal Home
With experienced dog-owning family in large country home who have time to spend with the dog, teaching it cart-pulling and sledding and giving obedience training. Definitely not a dog for apartments or urban dwellers nor for the casual owner.

This breed can trace its origins back to Babylonian times and is still used as a shepherd dog in parts of Europe.

| # MASTIFF

The Mastiff, sometimes known as The Old English, would seem to be a fairly direct descendant of the Molossus war dogs. At one time they were keen hunters and herders of sheep and cattle, fast moving dogs intent on bringing down deer in the forest. The modern Mastiff is, in maturity, a slow moving, dignified dog of somewhat impassive bearing. Its capacity for loyalty, care and overwhelming devotion to its owner is legendary. This magnificent dog presents many problems of ownership. It is expensive from every angle, difficult to mate and breed from, and sheer size makes supervision of its every move necessary.

Size
Height about 75cm (30 inches);
weight about 81.6kg (180 lbs).

Colour
Brindle or fawn with black
muzzle.

Grooming
Minimal except for weekly brush
and polish.

Life Span
About 7 years.

Health Problems
Although short-lived, generally
healthy except for hip dysplasia
(breeding stock should be
screened) and possible eye
problems.

Plus Points
Superb guard, faithful and loyal
companion, dignified noble
appearance.

Minus Points
Too large and expensive to buy
and maintain for most people,
rearing from puppy to adulthood
requires specialist knowledge,
in youth can be boisterous with
children and older people.

Ideal Home
On large country estate or farm,
possibly country club, golf club
or hotel standing in capacious
grounds, where dog can take
exercise at its own pace or in
company of owner.

Related breeds
Bull Mastiff (bred from Mastiff
and old type Bulldog), once the
gamekeeper's assistant against
poachers. A wonderful breed,
quiet with owners and family but
not with intruders. The breed is
not long lived and is prone to
leukaemia; *Neopolitan Mastiff*,
an enormous guarding breed,
which presents a would-be
owner with many problems
through sheer size. Not for
novice ownership.

Young Mastiffs.

| **GREAT DANE**

Despite its name, this dog is not Danish, but of German origin where for many centuries it was used for boar hunting. Because of its colossal size combined with a gentle, graceful bearing, the Dane attracts attention wherever it goes. In fact, most adult Danes can be led by an elderly person or a child without problems, and this breed can have a useful role in helping disabled people to move about and in teaching babies to walk. They are spectacular, glamorous animals and yet unassuming and pleasant to live with. Puppies are always expensive. Buy with great care from an experienced breeder who will also want assurance from you that you are a fit person to own the breed. Get expert advice from your vet on rearing the puppy. The temptation is to cram it with food, making the body too heavy for the youthful bone structure and leading to severe orthopaedic problems. This breed can be difficult to socialize outside the home as they must have only minimal exercise up to nine months old.

Size

Height 75cm (30 inches) males; weight 54.4kg (120 lbs) males; bitches a little less; cropped ears in US.

Colours

Fawn, brindle, black, steel blue or harlequin (white with black torn patches over body).

Grooming

Minimal, except for regular brushing.

Life Span

About 8 years.

Health Problems

Not a long-lived breed, there are some potential health problems, notably 'wobbler' syndrome, hip dysplasia and other orthopaedic problems of hind leg and shoulder, tendency to bloat.

Plus Points

Distinctive appearance, docile and dependable, good guard, minimal grooming and coat shedding.

Minus Points

Expensive to buy and feed, difficult to rear well, needs lots of space, obedience training and plenty of exercise when adult.

Ideal Home

With mixed-age family with large house and fenced-in garden, preferably in country, who will give dog obedience training, space and care it needs.

SAINT BERNARD

The St Bernard is popularly known as the dog which spends a lot of time padding up and down mountains with small kegs of brandy around its neck and, in fact, the breed has been used as a rescue dog in the Alps since the seventeenth century. However, it was only in the 1880s when its role in aiding stranded travellers became known worldwide that the breed was named the St Bernard after the monastery in the Swiss Alps with which it was traditionally associated. The rough-coated variety of this breed is a relatively late development, not so well suited to mountain rescue work (ice clings to the long coat and hampers the dog) but certainly popular with pet owners. Although the St Bernard is the type of dog many people long to own, few people can provide the ideal environment for this powerful but gentle creature. Owning a St Bernard is a big undertaking in more ways than one.

Size
Minimum height 77.5cm (31 inches) UK, 68.7cm (27½ inches) US; male weight about 74.8kg (165 lbs).

Colours
Shades of red or brindle with white markings; two coat varieties – rough (long-haired) and smooth (short-haired).

Grooming
Minimal for smooth coats; for rough coats 20 minutes brushing and combing per day.

Life Span
7 to 8 years.

Health Problems
Some breeding stock prone to "wobbler" syndrome, eye disease and heart problems.

Rough-coated St Bernard

Plus Points
Magnificent animal usually of equable temperament, slow moving and lethargic, exercise needs moderate viz. short, daily walks, patient, sympathetic companion for children.

Minus Qualities
Expensive to buy and maintain, breed has low sexual drive so difficult to mate, some drooling when eating and drinking, low tolerance to hot weather, warm rooms and cars.

Ideal Home
With experienced, dog-owning family on landed estate or similar, where this large and powerful dog can be housed correctly and have lots of room to move about. Definitely not a dog for apartment or urban life.

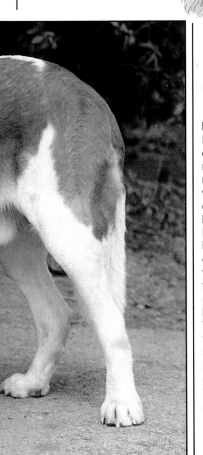

The Newfoundland is primarily a water dog, and one of its major drawbacks is that it is difficult to keep out of any kind of water – from tiny fish ponds to great lakes. The fishermen of Newfoundland trained these dogs to haul boats and carry nets and messages to the shore, and this bear-like dog will still perform these tasks if given the slightest opportunity. Newfoundland breed clubs often hold water trials for the dogs, sometimes lasting over a weekend when owners and dogs camp around a lake and really enjoy their dogs' very special talents. The 19th-century British painter, Sir Edwin Landseer, immortalized the black/white coloured variety of this breed which now bears his name. This is an extremely large dog of excellent temperament, very good with children, easy to teach but with little guarding ability.

Size
Height 70cm (28 inches); weight to 68kg (150 lbs) males, to 54kg (120 lbs) bitches.

Colours
Black, Landseer (black/white) or brown.

Grooming
Swimming in fresh water keeps coat in good condition; salt water must be washed out as it irritates the skin; keep ears dry and clean.

Life Span
About 9 years.

Health Problems
Generally healthy; breeding stock should be screened for hip dysplasia; heart disease, arthritis; puppies should be purchased only from experienced, reputable breeder.

Plus Points
Good-natured, especially kind to children, equable with other pets.

Minus Points
Must have regular access to swimming facilities, dog nearly always wet, greasy undercoat, exposed after heavy coat shedding in summer, can soil carpets and furnishings, some drooling when eating and drinking, expensive to buy and maintain.

Ideal Home
With active family in country house with interest in water sports or boating, preferably with lake or river nearby. This dog needs an outdoor life. Definitely not suitable for apartments or urban dwellings.

PUPPY CARE

Getting a puppy is always exciting but it is such an important event for you and your family, and heartbreaking if the wrong choice is made, that it is best done slowly over weeks or even months, if necessary. As suggested at the end of Chapter 3 *Where to buy a dog*, it is best to contact a reputable breeder of your chosen breed and find out when a litter is born. Before the litter arrives, it is wise to visit the breeder and look at the bitch, also possibly the stud dog so that you may examine parental temperament and perhaps other dogs of the same line. If you are impressed by both the breeder and his dogs, plan to see the litter at about 4-5 weeks old to make a choice.

Selecting the pup

It cannot be stressed too heavily that if you are seeking a companion dog all emphasis should be put upon temperament. It is foolish to let colour or markings be your overriding criteria. Be prepared to alter your mind about colour but do not be persuaded to change your original choice on sex.

You will already have formed some impressions about the breeder, the cleanliness of the premises, the amount of care the puppies have had, and possibly about the amount of mental stimulation available. A very tidy, empty but clean run may indicate that the pups are deprived of the activity which allows them to develop their mental and physical skills. Pups which can only play by pulling at each other's ears may develop into bullies or cowed individuals. The ideal puppy environment should contain some cardboard boxes to form tunnels, and to climb on, some toys to gnaw and something to pull between two pups.

Assessing temperament: The standard advice is to choose the puppy which comes towards you, but this can be a mistake, especially in a strong breed. The eager, pushy puppy may be one which later seeks to dominate its owner.

Jack Russell puppies in portable play pen

As a companion dog, you require a well-adjusted puppy, inquisitive and steady, but not the underdog of the litter nor the pack leader. Test the puppy's temperament by the way it reacts to minor stresses, such as being picked up, turned on to its back, having its face lightly blown into and pulled down gently on the ears. You should be able to handle the puppy, even slightly roughly, without any struggle. If, at the outset, the pup responds badly, it is already challenging human domination and this bodes ill for the future. The reactions of puppies when put into mildly unpleasant situations shows up extremes of temperament and these vary slightly from breed to breed. Toy breeds are sometimes babyish and will make a great deal of fuss about a minor upset, while dogs such as the Labrador will put up with a great deal of stress.

Age to buy

Modern thinking has it that a puppy is best left with the dam and its litter until 10-12 weeks of age. Not only will the pup be ready for its primary vaccinations as soon as it goes to its new owner but it will also have learned a great deal about the outside world from its dam and the rest of the litter and it will be starting to cope on its own. It is not until 12 weeks old that a puppy sleeps right through the night. Before this, it needs one or two play breaks and consequent urination and elimination breaks during the hours of darkness. Obviously, the slightly older puppy is therefore less trouble to its new owner at night.

However, these advantages are negated unless the breeder has been able to spend a considerable time on puppy education and has also given the puppies experience of alternate environments and ample space, as well as proper health care.

Health check on the new puppy

Never agree to take a puppy which is in less than perfect health. It is the breeder's responsibility to make sure the puppy is totally fit before it is sold. Firstly, note the puppy's general condition. If it is alert, with bright eyes and glossy coat, this is a good sign; puppies sitting hunched and miserable should make you highly suspicious of their health. The ideal puppy should feel heavy and full and should not be notably smaller or larger than the rest of the litter.

- Check the litter in its playpen, taking note of faeces passed. Pools of diarrhoea, even if only from one puppy, is an indication of ill-health; and check *your* puppy for signs of diarrhoea around the tail area.

- Check the puppy for hernias (lumps around the navel or in the groin); it is the breeder's responsibility to correct this condition but the operation can be risky and expensive.

- Check the puppy's urine; it should be directed away from the body so as not to scald the abdomen and there should not be a constant leak of urine.

- Check the eyes for mucus discharge, soreness and bald patches around the eye socket.

- Check the coat carefully: a loose dull coat may mean that the puppy is dehydrated and ill; look for spots on the abdomen and bald patches on the dam or puppies; check for black dust (flea excreta) at the lower end of the back in front of the tail and for scurf.

- If the tail has been docked, check that the end is healing properly and that hair is growing over the tip.

- Check for clean ears, without smell, and look for lice on the margins of the ears (although undesirable, lice are not a serious problem as long as they are treated by a veterinary surgeon as soon as possible).

- Check the puppy's hearing by taking it aside and dropping a metal object behind it.

- Check that the puppy can walk well (at 4 weeks) and run (at 6 weeks); move each limb to check for pain.

- Check for four toes on each foot, ensuring that the nails are cut short (ask the breeder how to clip nails so that you can continue to do this).

- Check the puppy's breathing: unless the weather or room is very hot, there should be no panting, or gurgles and rumbles in the chest.

- Watch the puppy feeding, making sure it can deal with reasonably-sized pieces of food easily; liquid should not blow back down the nose; check for vomiting soon after eating.

- Check the puppy's responses: put it down, attract its attention and see if it will come towards you, then follow you when you walk away.

- Check level of activity: an 8-week old puppy should play vigorously for at least 15 minutes before tiring; a 12-week old should continue for an hour or more.

Breeder's responsibilities

Having chosen your puppy, ask the breeder to put an identification tag around its neck. If you are not taking the puppy with you, expect to pay a reasonable deposit with the remainder paid when you take delivery of the pup. Your agreement with the breeder must include a full refund of the purchase price if a veterinary surgeon, examining the puppy as soon as it comes into your possession, advises that it will not make a good companion dog because of physical or temperamental disabilities. The breeder should also provide you with other information that documents the puppy's medical history and family background.

- Check how many times the puppy has been wormed, the dates on which it was done and the preparation used. Pass this information on to your veterinary surgeon.

- Ensure that the breeder provides you with a signed copy of the dog's pedigree and that registration application or certificate, transferring the puppy to you, is furnished at the time of sale.

- Check if insurance is available and if the puppy is insured. In many countries, breeders provide short-term insurance which covers the new owner for veterinary fees if the puppy is ill or injured in the first weeks of new ownership. Should the puppy die, there is a full refund of the purchase price. Where available, most responsible breeders offer this type of insurance which costs very little.

- Ask for a diet sheet indicating what, how and when the puppy is fed and what alterations need to be made as the puppy grows (discuss diet needs with your vet).

- Ask about your pup's grooming needs and the right tools to buy for the task. If yours is a coated breed, agree to contact the breeder for further advice as the puppy grows.

Vaccinations

Several infectious canine diseases caused by viruses and bacteria can be prevented, or at least rendered very mild by vaccination and regular boosting of the antibodies against the disease. When a large proportion of the dog population is protected against a disease, the illness may be rarely seen. But when vaccination is neglected, the disease will resurface, as with canine distemper in Britain.

The principle of vaccination is to introduce the puppy to disease in a safe fashion, so that antibodies are formed in its blood which will mobilize and protect it if the actual disease is encountered.

Puppies are born with a certain amount of protection acquired from their dam and take more from their mother's milk in the first few days of life. A puppy which has been hand-reared because the dam died or her milk failed will therefore be more vulnerable to infection.

The protection given by the dam wanes gradually and is usually almost gone by the time the puppy is 12-14 weeks old. This is the stage when the puppy is ready for vaccination and should respond readily. The veterinary surgeon will tell you what diseases the puppy should be protected against and how many injections should be given, and if any local skin reaction is to be expected. Vaccination is usually quite painless, and simply involves a hypodermic injection under the skin of the neck.

Antibodies are not created immediately, but take about 14-21 days to appear in the blood, so you must keep your puppy in isolation for the length of time the vet advises. If you wish to check that the requisite level of antibodies has been reached, a small amount of blood can be painlessly withdrawn from a vein in the front leg by your vet, and sent to a laboratory for assessment.

Your veterinary surgeon will also advice you when boosters are necessary, such as when the dog is just over a year old, and at intervals throughout its life. Certain vaccines, like that against kennel cough, are usually given shortly before a dog goes into a boarding kennel. This infection, which is more annoying than dangerous except in the very old or the very young, is most likely to be contracted where a number of dogs are mixed together in a confined space.

Your veterinary surgeon

Veterinary surgeons are not difficult to find, but perhaps the best way to find a suitable vet is to seek the advice and recommendations of pet-owning friends. There are many advantages in making the acquaintance of a veterinary surgeon before you buy your puppy. You may be directed to a reliable local breeder, and the vet will be able to tell you what are the weaknesses or hereditary conditions in the breed of your choice. You can also arrange for a health check and make plans for vaccinations in the light of the vet's local knowledge of the diseases current in the area.

When you have taken the puppy to the vet you will be expected to pay for the dog's treatment before leaving the surgery. The cost can be extremely high. If insurance is available for unexpected veterinary fees for emergency accidents and illness it is wise for any pet owner to invest in this. If you buy an insured puppy from the breeder, you will usually be offered permanent cover by the insurance company. Otherwise, ask at the veterinary surgery for proposal leaflets from the leading insurers.

Few veterinary surgeons make house calls nowadays but it is worth asking if home visits are ever possible. Inquire also how your first visit with the puppy will be stage managed: some vets run a type of casualty clinic, where you and your dog wait your turn; others have the more preferable appointment system. Veterinary fees vary greatly but more expensive tariffs may indicate that better-trained lay staff are employed, that in-patient care is better, and that there is more modern equipment and high-grade facilities. Inquire about the cost of some of the more common treatments and if you find the veterinary surgeon is friendly and willing to talk, then you are halfway to forming a good and lasting professional relationship.

First few nights

The first few nights in a new home are often long, lonely and chilly for your new puppy. Coming from the warmth and familiarity of a litter of pups into a strange environment is a disturbing experience and it is up to you to treat it at this critical time with sympathy and care.

● Let the puppy sniff about and familiarize itself with its new home.

Norfolk Terrier puppy

- Show the puppy its bed. This can be a basket lined with an old woollen garment or warm cloth or one of the newer types of collapsible crates made of wire mesh which are particularly suitable for puppies indoors (see opposite). Let the puppy examine it and get used to it.

- If you are using a folding crate, erect it in the bedroom of a member of the household. Make sure the bedding area (in either basket or crate) is warm and comfortable; a rubber hot-water bottle is often recommended in these early days to soothe the pup and give it something to nestle against.

- Reassure and comfort the puppy before putting it to bed and ideally it should require nothing more until morning.

- Early rising must be the rule until the puppy is at least six months old; puppies stir at first light and the owner must be on hand to take it outside to urinate.

- If your puppy whines or howls in the first few nights, you may be briefly comforting but firm. On no account pick the puppy up and do not allow it to sleep on your own bed or one of your family's. Teaching your dog to behave well begins immediately it comes into your possession. If you allow the puppy on to your bed or cosset it during the night it will, quite logically, expect such behaviour to continue.

- Plan to move your puppy's crate or basket out of the bedroom and to its regular resting place in a draught-free, comfortable corner of the house after a few days or a little longer when the dog has developed confidence in you and your home.

Helping your puppy adjust

Your puppy learns to live as a companion dog the moment it comes into your home and it is your task to show that behaviour which was acceptable in the playpen with the rest of the litter is not suitable in your house. Do not ask too much at first; remember the puppy has a great deal of adjustment to make without the familiar sights, sounds, smells and support of the dam and litter. Give your puppy time to explore its new world and allow it to make its own decisions in some matters. The puppy has a lot to learn and it is up to you to make the lessons as painless as possible.

Teaching your puppy good behaviour

It is best to think of *teaching* your puppy, rather than training, which has harsh connotations. Puppies learn by trial and reward. If the puppy performs some action which gives it pleasure in one form or another, such as raiding a shopping bag left on your kitchen floor – then it will want to do so again, because the bag yielded objects to chew and probably something edible. The easiest way to teach a young puppy that this behaviour is not allowed is to put shopping bags and other possessions out of reach and to *train yourself* not to leave objects about which the puppy can get at. At this early stage, it would be wrong to punish a puppy for playing with objects left within reach but later on a stage is reached when the puppy is able to distinguish between what is permitted and what is not. Then, more positive teaching is appropriate, a task which is, incidentally, made much easier as the puppy becomes progressively less inquisitive.

Sleeping and playing areas

The best way to teach a puppy acceptable behaviour is to limit its world to an easily-cleaned area where someone can keep an eye on it for most of the time. There can be little sympathy for the owner who complains of the puppy making messes all over the house, simply because a puppy should not be allowed the freedom of the house and, unless strictly supervised, should be kept to the kitchen or utility room. This may mean that, in order to give the puppy sufficient company, family members will have to spend more time in the kitchen – but that is all part of having a new puppy.

Mesh dog crates: One of the best puppy-education aids in recent times is the wire-mesh collapsible crate which can be quickly erected wherever you want it. Buy a size suitable for an adult dog of your breed and you will find that the puppy quickly adjusts to what will become its permanent "dog house" – a secure den and cozy piece of territory for the dog, whether it is in the sitting room, erected beside a swimming pool, in a hotel room or even when travelling on a train.

The great advantage of the crate is that the door can be left open, so allowing the puppy to play outside the crate, or closed when necessary, such as when meals are being prepared or when workmen are in the house; the puppy can still be with human company, can see and be seen yet be protected from harm. One section of the crate can serve as the dog's sleeping area, which is preferable to shutting the puppy away behind a closed door at night.

Even a young puppy will avoid soiling its crate if at all possible so be alert when the puppy wakes from sleep to take it to its designated toilet area. A small puppy needs to urinate at least every two hours and will defecate after every meal, which is four or five times a day. Being aware and watchful of these basic needs is part of teaching the pup good manners and it will make little progress if it is obliged to soil its own territory because no one is on hand to take it out.

The puppy must also be allowed periods of free play on the floor, during which time it will explore its immediate surroundings. Supervise the puppy carefully in these periods; the use of the vital word 'no' begins here, together perhaps with a sharp handclap to emphasize behaviour that is definitely forbidden.

House-training

This is a matter of taking the puppy to a chosen place outdoors and remaining with it until it urinates or defecates. In training the dog, it is helpful to use a short word or phrase – "busy, busy" for example, is commonly used when training guide dogs for the blind – which can be repeated when necessary. It is essential that you remain with the dog and, preferably, educate it to use your chosen spot at once. However, many dog owners compromise by, at first, allowing the puppy to use any place outdoors, then progressing to the use of a special area. If your puppy *must* use a public place, do choose the spot with care, taking into consideration the rights of ordinary citizens to clean pavements and paths; if necessary, clean up after your dog. House-training a puppy can be boring and time-consuming, especially when the puppy is small, inquisitive and easily distracted but this stage soon passes and persistence wins out in the end.

Puppies of small breeds can be similarly trained to use newspaper or a cat tray indoors or on a balcony or patio. All puppies should be reliably house-trained by the age of six months. If your training has been consistent and your puppy is still not house-trained, consider checking its health with the vet.

Disciplining your puppy

When you discipline your puppy, use short sharp words and use them consistently; you will confuse the puppy if the rebuke is concealed in a flow of rhetoric. A firm "no" accompanied by a loud noise is far more effective than, for example, "No, you must not do that. I told you not to do that", but this correction should only be administered when the pup approaches a forbidden area or is actually doing something wrong. Dogs do not have moral values nor know instinctively the difference between right and wrong, only what they have been *taught* by their owner is acceptable or unacceptable. All dogs will be disobedient and mischievous at some time and they do seem to display guilt when caught red-handed in a disobedient act; this, however, does not prevent them from behaving in this way nor repeating such behaviour if given the opportunity.

Be patient and consistent, and kindly but firm when reprimanding a puppy and be prepared to repeat your

Puppies should respond to petting and handling by family members

rebukes often in the early stages until your dog knows what is permissible. Reinforce good behaviour by praising and rewarding your puppy with pats and hugs, and remember that very little is gained (and possible harm done) by physically punishing your puppy for "bad" behaviour. House soiling is an example, in which too often a dog is punished when human neglect or inattention in not letting the dog out is the real cause of the mess. In this situation, it is a cruelty to punish the dog, and the offending mess should be cleaned up without a word. Patience, repetition, practice and kind but firm handling, not force or bullying, are the factors which produce a well-behaved dog.

Come when called

It should always be a pleasure for your dog to come to you. The fact that it does so quickly and willingly may, at times, be crucial. The habit of wanting to come to its owner or a family member is easily established in a puppy, because almost universally puppies are eager to please and want to be petted. Get down to the puppy's level and call it to you by name with open arms. This is best done at first when the puppy is coming towards you anyway. Reward the puppy, as you do every time it behaves well, with pats and hugs and occasionally with a small morsel of food. The occasional food reward not only saves obesity but makes the puppy try harder to please in the hope that the biscuit will be given this time. Never use food consistently as a reward or the dog will expect it and fail to obey if food is not forthcoming.

As the puppy develops, practise calling it when further away and intent on some activity. It must be accepted that guarding and toy breeds will "come when called" more easily than gundog and scenting breeds which are, at times, almost dominated by their senses.

DEVELOPMENT AND BEHAVIOUR OF DOGS

Puppies are born quite unable to cope with life away from the dam (or mother). After an average pregnancy of 63 days, pups are born with undeveloped eyes and ears, teeth not through the gums and limbs unable to support the body. However, puppies can crawl and recognize the dam by scent, thus having a sure instinct for finding warmth and food.

Puppies grow rapidly, doubling their birth weight in seven days. A puppy weighing .38kg (12 oz) at birth will, in a medium to large breed, reach 4.5kg (10 lbs) by the time it is eight weeks of age. Many breeds do not show their true colour at birth and in some it may not be apparent until adolescence. Be guided by the breeder as to the eventual colour of your pup.

1-4 weeks: Eyes start to open when the puppy is 10-14 days old and the ears have developed and hearing is present by about 21-25 days when the pups will bark for the first time. After a few days in the litter, barking may cease and may not be heard again until the dog is almost adult. Weaning on to solid food takes place from 2½ weeks old, when the baby teeth are through. Most puppies can walk by 3½ weeks.

4-8 weeks: Most puppies should be running by five weeks. In medium to large breeds, seven-week-old puppies can be ready to go to new homes. In small to medium breeds, 12 weeks is the usual age for leaving the litter. For companion dogs, it is advisable to remove the pups to their new homes early because the dam begins to teach her puppies attack and defence skills which may be inappropriate for a household pet. Moreoever, puppies at this stage of their development are adventurous and bold and usually take the new experience in their stride, although some may undergo a short "fear" period because of the trauma of separation. Within seven days of changing ownership, the puppy should be responding to its name and should know the location of its bed and retire there voluntarily when tired.

At seven weeks, the healthy puppy should be able to eat

from a dish, to walk and run, balance on its hind quarters for defecation and be playful and willing to respond to gentle and friendly overtures from people. It will also require lots of sleep, having periods of furious activity for up to half-an-hour followed by about three hours sleep. It is very important that the puppy should not be roused, even to give visitors or children pleasure, as sleep builds steady nerves and good temperament.

At this stage, the puppy should be on four or five small meals a day, so it is demanding to take care of the young animal. The puppy's training and education should also begin at this age which means that a great deal of time must be spent with the puppy which, ideally, should hardly ever be left alone.

At four months: By this age, certain skills such as running, jumping, scenting, digging and carrying should be relatively well-developed. However, teething problems begin as the baby teeth are shed and the adult set of 42 teeth break through the gums. This causes the puppy a variable amount of pain which may be expressed by compulsive chewing on human hands or woodwork, by carrying the ear in the down position on the affected side and even by watering of the eye because of the related pain.

At six months: By this age, the normal puppy should be completely housetrained and on 2-3 meals a day. It should also be capable of walking on a lead and staying alone for periods of up to an hour during the day.

Adolescence and adulthood: Some small breeds will reach adult size and bearing when they are six months old, but large to giant breeds will not be fully grown until two years or even more. In adolescence, males of the larger breeds often challenge their owner's dominance. It is as well to be on guard for this challenge and to handle it quickly and firmly by making the dog strongly aware of its place in the family pecking order. Dogs which become unmanageable at this time all too frequently end up being destroyed.

It is possible for a bitch to come into oestrus (have her first heat or season) as early as six months old, but some will be 10 months, over one year, or almost two years. At this stage it may be useful to have her checked by a veterinary surgeon to see that all is normal. The interval between seasons is said to be six months, but many perfectly healthy bitches have eight or even 10 month intervals. Intervals shorter than six months are not a good sign and warrant a veterinary check.

Males are capable of siring a litter from about eight months old. A male pup should have two testicles visibly descended into the scrotum by three months old. Get veterinary advice if this has not happened, as it may be necessary to prepare yourself to have the retained testicle removed when the dog is about two years old, owing to the tendency for such a testicle to become cancerous. A dog that has only one descended testicle (popularly known as a monorchid) can sire puppies, although he will have reduced fertility, but a dog with two undescended testicles (a cryptorchid) cannot.

Urinating/territory marking: A male dog will start to urinate from the standing position (popularly known as "cocking his leg") at about a year old. This position is primarily used for marking territory and the dog may revert to the crouching position for urination at times, especially when ill or in old age.

Tail docking/ear cropping: In those breeds where tail docking is customary, this is done at 3-4 days old, usually by the breeder and without anaesthetic. Ear cropping is prohibited in Great Britain and a number of other countries; dogs with cropped ears may not be shown in the UK. Where cropping is accepted, it is done from the age of 10 weeks, depending on the breed, size, weight and condition of the puppy. After the surgery, the puppy wears a frame on its head for a time to train the now-cropped ears to stand upright in the approved manner.

Coat shedding: In most breeds, dogs shed their coat twice a year under natural conditions, but dogs kept in warm houses tend to shed all the year round. This can be a nuisance in certain circumstances. Dogs of the non-shedding breeds require regular grooming and, in most cases, trimming to maintain the correct appearance and keep the skin and coat healthy. The cost of professional grooming should be taken into account as a lifelong expense when considering a heavily groomed or trimmed breed.

Behaviour patterns

The basic patterns of behaviour are very much the same for all breeds of dogs.

Scent: Dogs communicate with each other mainly by scent, either by direct scent identification of other dogs, or by scent left on marking posts, mainly through urine. Dogs can determine, through scent, the sex, temper, pack status, intentions, and phase in the sexual cycle of every dog they encounter physically and also the dogs which have passed through their territory or over the ground on which they are exercised. Although scenting power is best in dogs with normal muzzles and wide nostrils, even those with the lowest scenting ability – the short-faced breeds (Bulldog,

Communication between dogs

Pekingese, etc.) – have a thousand times the scenting ability of man. Maximum scent identification also involves licking, as the main scent organ lies in the roof of the mouth.

Dogs issue scent from glands situated under the tail, and from the urine, as well as from the sweat glands in the feet. It is thought that the scent quality of the urine alters with the sexual cycle and with the temper. Male dogs direct a stream of urine periodically at marking posts within their territory, and they will re-mark these sites if another dog has marked them. It is possible that this marking urine has different scent from that passed normally.

Body language: Dogs also use body language to convey their temper and intent to others. The way the ears are carried, a movement of the lips, arching or relaxation of the body and the way the tail is held can be "read" by other dogs and to some extent by humans. The broad band of hair which runs down the centre back contains erector muscles, which can bring the hair upright, making the dog look bigger when it is angry.

Eye contact: This is an important means of communication between dogs and between dogs and humans. A direct stare constitutes a challenge, while averted eyes display a desire to avoid a confrontation. An aggressive dog should not be stared at directly, but it is pleasant for an owner to meet the eyes of his dog and watch the softening, almost smiling expression which enters them when the owner's approval is assured.

Modifying puppy behaviour: Puppies do not have total command of this canine language, but signs of it are there, and it is important to quell any of the aggressor signs when they are used against humans, even by a tiny puppy. Fortunately, puppies are easy to dominate in the way that a superior dog would, either by holding the puppy by the loose skin at the back of the neck and giving a gentle shake, or by holding the puppy down and pressing its head to the ground. Both these methods should be applied by the owner to subdue any attempt on the part of a puppy to challenge human authority. This type of domination cannot be used in other areas of puppy education, such as housetraining, which is entirely a requirement of domestication and not part of essential pack manners.

Development of a dog

At birth
Ears and eyes undeveloped, unable to stand, scenting power very strong. Urination and defecation only induced by licking by the bitch.

7-10 days
Birthweight doubled. Eyes developed and opening, but non-focusing.

3-6 weeks
Can hear and see well, bark, eat semi-solid food, has milk teeth. Can run and begins to play.

6-8 weeks
Urination and defecation of own volition.

8-14 weeks
May experience "fear" period owing to adjustments, including separation from dam and litter, new environment with human family. Becomes vulnerable to virus diseases as maternal antibody wanes. Eats solid food. Housetraining begins but has little bladder control.

14-20 weeks
Vaccination programme completed, so can be taken out on public ground. Increasing skills include running, jumping, scenting, digging, carrying. Greater control of urination but not dry all night. Ears may "fly" while nerves of the face are affected by cutting the permanent teeth. Great need to chew and gnaw. Tolerance to cow's milk may end. Fluffy puppy coat is shed and adult coat begins to come through, often with colour change. Lead training for small breeds.

20-40 weeks
Housetraining perfected, but may regress in illness or a stress situation. Exercise for large and giant breeds starts at 24 weeks. Puberty may begin, dog and bitch capable of breeding.

40-52 weeks
Bids for domination may be made by males in aggressive breeds. Education should be reinforced.

1 year to 18 months
Booster vaccination needed. Full growth achieved in all but giant breeds. Maximum capability for running, jumping and maximum need for companionship and activity.

It is wrong to think dogs eat only meat. During thousands of years of domestication dogs have come to eat very much as their owners do, except that they do not need to vary their diet, nor do they need highly spiced foods or the remnants of meals intended for humans.

Nutritional needs

A dog's food must include protein (meat, fish, eggs, cheese, soy beans) for growth and for repair of the body tissues, but a diet of unadulterated meat will kill a dog in a relatively short time.

Dogs need a high proportion of carbohydrate (cooked wheat or maize (corn), bread, dog biscuit, rice or pasta) for energy and to keep warm. Fat is also needed for energy, to provide warmth, to give good palatability, to keep the coat in good condition and to carry essential fatty acids required for important bodily functions. Fat is provided by the fat content of meat (absolutely lean meat does not suit dogs), corn or sunflower oil, butter or margarine. The diet must also contain fibre, to keep the digestive organs active, and the correct proportion of minerals and vitamins to help break down and facilitate the digestion of food. Water is also an essential for life and must always be available to the dog, and not replaced by milk or other liquid.

These nutritional requirements can be provided for your dog in a number of ways, even on a vegetarian regime, but the important fact to assimilate is that once you have found a diet which suits your dog in terms of good digestive function and satisfactory growth, and which suits you, in terms of buying, storing and feeding, then the dog should be given this diet every day. Changes of menu do not suit dogs, but if changes must be made, they should be achieved gradually over at least 2-3 weeks.

Feeding puppies

Puppies of eight weeks old need to be fed 4-5 times a day. According to breed and growth rate, a puppy may be able to take enough food to be satisfied and grow well at three meals by the time it is 14 weeks old. Three meals are usually continued through the first winter and then, if the dog no longer seems to need a mid-day meal, it can progress to simply a morning and evening meal. This regime is preferable to the "one meal a day" feeding programme which used to be advised.

Keep the puppy on the diet recommended by the breeder for at least the first two weeks in your home. Then, if you wish to change the puppy's diet to, say, canned or dried food, do so gradually, substituting only a little of the new type of food at first. Beware of trying to cram or force-feed a puppy, especially in the larger breeds. It can be dangerous to try to accelerate growth and to make the puppy too heavy for its limbs.

Puppies need roughly twice as much food per day as an adult dog of the same body weight. A toy breed may be "adult" at six months old; a large breed – for example, a Rottweiler – may not be "adult" (that is, achieved puberty and be fully grown) until almost two years old. It is normal for an adolescent dog in the large breeds to look lean and to show the outline of the ribs. This is far better than it being too heavy at this age. The daily calorie requirements of a growing puppy and of an adult dog are shown below. Note that many puppies and adult dogs require more food than adult humans.

Daily calorie requirements for puppies and adults

Weight	Puppy	Adult
9kg (2 lbs)	265 cals	130 cals
3kg (6½ lbs)	625 cals	300 cals
6.8kg (15 lbs)	1100 cals	550 cals
11.3kg (25 lbs)	1675 cals	800 cals
15.8kg (35 lbs)	2200 cals	1050 cals
18.1kg (40 lbs)	2400 cals	1200 cals
27.2kg (60 lbs)	3300 cals	1575 cals
36.3kg (80 lbs)	4050 cals	2000 cals
45.3kg (100 lbs)	4900 cals	2400 cals

Types of dog food

Nutritionally satisfactory meals for dogs can be given in a number of ways but it cannot be emphasized too much that the food given must please the owner and the dog, because the giving of food is one of the most important elements of the dog and owner relationship. The owner that feels repugnance at handling or storing the dog's food will not create a satisfactory bond between himself and his pet. Among the basic types of dog food are:

- **Home cooked/prepared:** Fresh meat, (cooked or raw), cereal and plain kibbled dog biscuit or cereal (bread, rice, pasta) plus vitamin/mineral supplement.

- **Home cooked/prepared:** Eggs, cheese or fish in place of meat, with biscuit or cereal, plus vitamin/mineral supplement.

- **Commercial dog food plus cereal:** Top-quality canned dog food plus dog biscuit or cereal.

- **Commercial dog food:** Canned food, nutritionally complete.

- **Commercial dog food:** Dry foods in pellet or loose form which are fed with a small amount of protein for puppies, and always with ample water.

- **Foods to avoid:** Inferior quality ready-ground meat, sausage-type preserved meats, milk after the age of six months, oily fish in quantity, spices.

Advantages of canned dog food

There can be no doubt that good-quality canned dog foods are the most convenient way of feeding the companion dog. These foods are nutritionally balanced and contain sufficient vitamins and minerals for the dog's needs, so there is no guesswork involved in dosage of supplements and no extra expense. This is, however, an expensive way of feeding the larger breeds. Canned foods (and dry dog foods) should be fed according to manufacturer's directions. Read the labels carefully. The various flavours are provided to attract the dog owner.

Vitamin and mineral supplements

At times of rapid growth, or after illness, your veterinary surgeon may prescribe additional vitamin/mineral supplements. If the dog's food is home made, a good vitamin/mineral supplement is strongly advised, since such food is rarely perfectly balanced nutritionally. Particular care should be taken when using codliver oil. Ask your veterinary surgeon about the dosage, which should be in drops rather than spoonfuls, as considerable harm may be done to the skeleton by giving too much.

Food precautions

Eggs should always be cooked. Potatoes are a good dog food if well cooked. Milk may prove too laxative for many adult dogs. Liver and kidney should only be fed in small quantities as this also is laxative.

Sample menus for a 6.8kg (15 lb) growing puppy, or a 15.8kg (35 lb) adult dog (eg. Brittany):

MENU 1
Daily ration, divided into two meals. 150g (5 oz) raw meat, plus 150g (5 oz) plain dog biscuit, plus vitamin/mineral supplement.

MENU 2
100g (4 oz) cooked beef, plus 100g (4 oz) bread, plus 50g (2 oz) dog biscuit in the evening plus vitamin/mineral supplement.

MENU 3
225g (8 oz) raw tripe, plus 100g (4 oz) boiled rice, plus vitamin/mineral supplement; evening, 2 cooked eggs plus 2 slices of brown bread.

MENU 4
1½ cans of good-quality canned food plus an equal volume of dog biscuit.

MENU 5
2½ cans of canned dog food which includes cereal.

MENU 6
For vegetarians, 100g (4 oz) oatmeal porridge, 300ml (½ pint) milk, 225g (8 oz) cottage cheese; evening, 2 boiled eggs, 3 slices of bread, 150g (5 oz) can baked beans.

MENU 7
225g (8 oz) minced chicken, 225g (8 oz) boiled potatoes; evening 50g (2 oz) Cheddar cheese, 2 slices bread, 2 sweet biscuits.

Boxer puppies feeding

Calorie guide

25g (1 oz) butter/margarine	226 cals
1 cooked egg	80 cals
100g (4 oz) boiled rice	150 cals
50g (2 oz) mature cheese	240 cals
1 slice bread	80 cals
100g (4 oz) pasta, cooked	115 cals
1 small sweet biscuit	40 cals
100g (4 oz) dog biscuit	420 cals
100g (4 oz) raw beef	500 cals
100 g(4 oz) cooked beef	300 cals

HEALTH CARE

There are a number of common dog diseases and potential health problems which every dog owner should know about. Watch your dog carefully for early signs of illness or disease. As always, prompt action can often prevent serious complications.

Worms

Dogs, in common with most other animals, provide a shelter and good living for a number of parasitic worms. Almost every puppy is born with a burden of the **roundworm** (*Toxocara canis*) acquired from its dam while in the uterus and via the milk she provides. While breeders do try to have their bitches as worm-free as possible, and will also work towards freeing the puppies of worms from the age of 2½ weeks, it is virtually impossible for any dog to be truly worm free. Although there may be no evidence of worms, the very nature of a dog's habits – such as sniffing and eating grass and ground on which parasite eggs lie, smelling the rectal area of other dogs (one of their prime methods of communication) – mean that the army of parasites survives most successfully, despite all the aids of modern science. Because most parasitical worms are harmful to the dog, and some can be harmful to humans, particularly children, it is important to keep dogs, and most especially puppies, as free as possible of worms.

When you buy your puppy, ask the breeder what worming has been done, and pass this information to the vet when you take the puppy for its vaccination. Ask your vet to furnish a schedule of worming to be administered.

Children run the most risk of picking up and swallowing *Toxacara* eggs, which can lead to permanent loss of vision if *Toxocara* larvae become embedded behind the eye. However, *Toxocara* is one of the rarest diseases transmitted from animals to man and if parents and dog owners take a number of simple precautions there should be little danger from this infection.

- Pay special attention to worming puppies often.

- Pick up and dispose of dog faeces properly.

- Insist that children wash hands and faces after handling a puppy.

- Do not allow dogs to eat off crockery used by humans.

- Keeping long-haired puppies well groomed especially around the hind quarters.

- Always use an effective worming preparation in dosages suitable for the body weight of the dog.

Ask your veterinary surgeon's advice on the worming preparation to use. Modern vermifuges are painless, palatable, and do not involve pre-starvation. You are unlikely to see any worms expelled, except in young puppies, as modern preparations kill adult worms inside the body and they are passed out unnoticed in the faeces. However, the egg and larval stage of many worms is difficult to destroy, so the cycle of the parasite will continue, but in a reduced population. *Toxacara canis* larvae never develop into adult worms in the human body and this is *not* the same infection as roundworms in children.

Tapeworms in the dog are associated with fleas which harbour the parasite at one stage in its life-cycle. Dogs which carry fleas are therefore at special risk from tapeworm, which can cause digestive problems in the dog. **Heartworm** is a problem for dogs which live in tropical areas of mosquito infestation and they must be regularly treated for this. Your veterinary surgeon will advise about heartworm, if necessary.
   If you are worried about the incidence of worms in your pet, (cats have worms, too) and want maximum protection for small children, your veterinary surgeon will be able to have a worm count done on a small sample of faeces for quite low cost. This will give a reliable guide to the amount and type of worm infestation your animals have.

External parasites
Dogs, especially heavy-coated dogs, prove a home for a number of parasites which live in and upon the skin. Fleas are the most prolific, but lice, harvest mites, cheyletiella, ticks and mange mites all cause trouble, and may well be the cause of skin infection in the dog, as well as being transmitted to sensitive humans. Any dog can pick up any of these parasites and many are acquired by walking through long grass.

Fleas: Most dog fleas come from either domestic or feral cats, which have deposited their fleas where they lie. Unfortunately, the flea population is on the increase, helped by the modern trend to install heating and wall-to-wall carpeting in houses. Fleas breed all the year round in houses and, in fact, spend little time actually on animals. However, the bite of just one flea can cause a severe allergic reaction in many dogs and persistent itching which the dog can turn into self-inflicted wounds through scratching. On the other hand, some dogs will tolerate a huge colony of fleas without any irritation. Thorough daily grooming is the start of a campaign against fleas. Look for the tell-tale black powder which is flea faeces, found most often on the back of the dog, in front of the tail. This substance, which looks like coal dust, is readily identified if combed out onto damp paper, when it will give a red stain.

Baths are not much use against fleas, but the dog (and domestic cats) should be well sprayed with an effective anti-flea preparation. In addition, it is particularly important to treat upholstered furniture, edges of carpets, the dog's bed and any other places it may lie, with a special environmental spray. Treatment should be repeated as frequently as the manufacturer recommends. Your veterinary surgeon will advise you of effective preparations.

One word of warning: If you find fleas on your dog do not immediately put on a flea collar and hang anti-parasite strips around its bed, as well as treating dog and environment with anti-flea powder. These preparations contain powerful chemicals and there can be a build-up if too many are used at once. Regular precautions rather than an intensive campaign are advised.

Lice: These are spread from dog to dog or cat to dog, and are most frequently seen around the ear margins of young puppies, where a heavy infection can cause anaemia. Your veterinary surgeon will identify lice on his first examination of your puppy and will advise on eradication.

Ticks: These are spread to dogs from wild animals and livestock, usually from grass. A tick is invisible when first acquired by the dog, but as it engorges itself with blood it becomes larger and redder, resembling a small tumour or skin tag. The dog does not appear to feel the ticks unless there are a great number on the skin, but when thoroughly engorged, ticks will drop off and leave a blood stain, possibly on the carpet or floor. Remove ticks by swabbing with surgical spirit and then pulling out smartly with tweezers. Try not to leave the head and mouthparts in the dog's skin.

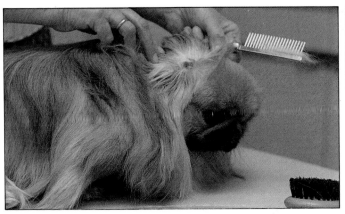

Examining Pekingese's ears for infection

Cheyletiella: These are very small mites which look like scurf down the spine of a dog. This mite is most often seen on smooth-coated breeds such as Dachshunds and Boxers, and it can be transmitted to humans, causing an irritating rash in the midriff area. A medicated bath obtained from the vet will clear the dog of the mite; the rash on humans should clear spontaneously.

Harvest mites (*Trombicula Autumnalis*): These are very tiny, bright orange mites picked up in the countryside around harvest time. They tend to infest the dog's feet causing intense itching, and will also cause a painful scarlet rash on exposed skin of feet and legs in humans. Seek veterinary advice for a suitable preparation to use.

Mange mites and ear mites: Both cause extreme irritation to the dog, and if this is allowed to continue, the dog will scratch itself raw, creating an even worse skin condition. Ask your veterinary surgeon to show you how to keep the dog's ears clean. Suspect ear mites if the ears smell unpleasant and have a reddish brown deposit inside.

Hairless patches on legs or feet, or round the muzzle, may indicate the presence of mange mites, which can lead to a serious condition. See the veterinary surgeon immediately for a positive diagnosis and suitable treatment.

Signs of illness

Disinclination to play or take part in household activities, together with refusal of food, is often the first indication of illness in the dog. For a very young puppy in this state, get veterinary advice straight away. An older puppy may be left 12 hours to see if the condition persists and an adult dog can wait 24 hours. The dog must be offered or persuaded to take water, or glucose water (1 tablespoonful to 600 ml [1 pint] of boiled water) because dehydration complicates any illness.

Poisons: If you suspect that your dog has eaten some poisonous substance, (many household cleaners, and garden chemicals and pesticides are poisonous) take the dog to the vet immediately and take with you any torn packages or similar evidence. Some common poisons are: old lead paint, car antifreeze, paint remover, detergents, slug killers, rat and mouse poisons, bulbs, daffodil and snow drops, some common plants if chewed, (e.g. laburnum twigs, poppy seed heads) and some house plants.

Vomiting and diarrhoea: These probably cause most worry to pet owners. Either may clear up within a few hours or they may be the first indication of a more serious problem. Watch the dog carefully for clues to the possible cause and note any other symptoms in order to report to the vet. You can always ask for advice on the telephone.

Mild vomiting as the result of eating putrid food may be treated with 24-hour starvation, but always allow access to water. If the dog vomits after drinking, the water intake must be controlled. Remove all water bowls, flower vases, etc that the dog can reach and give water in very small quantities at hourly intervals. If there is not improvement within a few hours, take the dog to the vet.

Diarrhoea is often the natural consequence of unwise eating, or it can be the beginning of a serious infection. Blood in or on the faeces is cause for alarm. Keep a chart of the number of times the dog defecates, whether there is evidence of straining or pain, and possibly take a sample of the faeces to help the vet in his diagnosis. Diarrhoea with lethargy, refusal to eat, and a cold clammy feel to the skin is obviously more serious than diarrhoea in a dog which is still running about and willing to eat. Exercise the same kind of judgement with the sick dog as you would with a child, remembering, however, that dogs hardly ever fake illness to get out of disagreeable duties.

Canine parvovirus: This is a relatively new dog disease which first appeared almost simultaneously in several parts of the world in 1978. It is characterized by sudden heart failure in very young puppies, or by violent haemorrhagic diarrhoea and vomiting in the older puppy or adult dog. Puppies from 4-12 months are the most vulnerable, and there is still a disquieting number of deaths even in puppies which have been vaccinated against CPV. Because antibodies against this disease received by the puppy from its dam last a long time, it is difficult to know when precisely to give CPV vaccinations. The virus itself is difficult to destroy with disinfectants and lingers in the environment where it is spread by dogs which have or are incubating the disease. To make really certain that your puppy is ready for CPV vaccination, your veterinary surgeon can first take a blood test, but this will add to your costs. Many vets advise giving two shots or more of CPV vaccine in order to give maximum protection.

Nettle rash (hives): Many puppies, especially smooth-coated ones, may suffer from nettle rash (hives) in their first summer due to contact with plants, or some other irritating substance. A small dose of antihistamine tablets (obtainable without prescription from pharmacists) is an effective treatment for this generally minor condition, except in the very short-nosed breeds when the breathing may be obstructed, and veterinary help may be needed.

Wasp and bee stings: If you can see the sting, pull it out with tweezers. Meat tenderizer (papain) will reduce the swelling and ease the pain. Stings are only dangerous when in the mouth or throat area, or where the facial area threatens to swell violently. In this case, take the dog to the vet at once.

Heat stroke: Dogs can only lower their body heat by panting, or via the few sweat glands in the feet. These relatively inefficient cooling methods mean that the dog is at risk from heat stroke in hot weather or if confined in an unventilated, unshaded place, such as a closed car, or a small kennel or even a hot room. A dog left in a car with the windows slightly open can be in grave danger of heat stroke, even in slightly cool weather unless there is some boost to the air circulation, such as an electric fan. The overheated dog should be cooled as quickly as possible. Drape cold, wet towels over the head and chest or pour water over the dog or dunk it in a bath or trough of cold water or in a stream (beware of drowning an unconscious dog). If nothing else is available, packs of frozen food may be placed round the dog. Do not immerse the dog in water for too long, as this can make its temperature abnormally low. When the dog has revived, take it to a veterinary surgeon as quickly as possible.

Faints: Dogs of the short-nosed breeds may faint in hot weather or on sudden exertion. If walking with the dog, it is usually sufficient to sit down in a cool, shaded place for a short time, allowing the dog complete rest until it revives. If water is available, cool the dog as above, but without total immersion which is unnecessary in this case.

Fits: A surprising number of dogs are epileptic. Others have occasional fits for no apparent reason. Fits usually take place during the evening or the early morning while the dog is asleep. It is rare for a dog to have a fit while out walking, or in the show ring, or while engaged in any other activity. There is little that can be done while the dog is in a fit, except to protect it from such injuries as rolling into a fire or down stairs. Keep the atmosphere quiet, turn off radios and television and avoid any loud noise or shouting. Make a note of how long the fit lasted and of any unusual behaviour in the dog before the onset of the fit. There is no point in getting the vet to a dog in a fit, or even making an immediate call when the dog has recovered, but it is wise to report the occurrence to the vet in the next few days. In the majority of cases, the dog recovers within minutes and, although it may seem a little dazed, is probably unaware that anything unusual has happened. With carefully regulated medication, dogs live for many years even if epilepsy is diagnosed. If, however, the first fit is followed quickly by another, the situation is immediately more serious and the vet should be telephoned at once.

Cut pads and other injuries: Pads and ear flaps bleed excessively and out of all proportion to the extent of the injury. Staunch the bleeding with large amounts of cotton cloth held firmly onto the wound. If the dog has a small wound, it may be allowed to lick and clean itself, but any wounds more than 2.5cm (1 inch) long should be seen to by a vet.

Rabies: Great Britain and Australasia are among the few countries in the world to be free of indigenous rabies, the deadly disease for which there is no effective treatment, and which can be fatal for dogs and humans alike. In other countries, puppies must be vaccinated against rabies at 12-16 weeks with booster shots every year. Because it is rabies-free, it is not permissible for dogs to enter the UK from abroad without first undergoing a six-months quarantine (at the owner's expense) – a warning which UK pet owners travelling abroad, as well as pet-owning visitors to the UK, should heed.

General care of the dog

There are several excellent books available on dog health, nursing and first aid and responsible dog owners should have one of these on their book shelves. Especially recommended are *Dog Owner's Home Veterinary Handbook* (Howell House, New York) and *Doglopaedia* by J. M. Evans MRCVS and Kay White (Henston Ltd, Friary Court, 13-21 High Street, Guildford, Surrey, GU1 3DX) and *The Dog Care Question & Answer Book* by Dr Barry Bush BVSc, PhD, FRCVS (Orbis Publishing).

Puppies are subject to all kinds of minor illnesses and accidents in the first few months of life, mainly through their

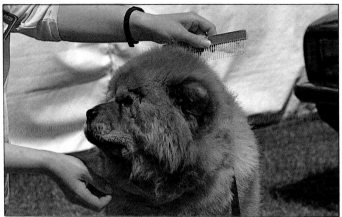

Chow Chows and other thick-coated breeds need regular grooming

own natural curiosity and desire to explore and sample things. Keep a very careful watch on small puppies both indoors and out and keep household cleansers and other toxic substances well out of reach. With young puppies you need to take all the safety precautions in the home that you would with a young child.

Lost dog: Dogs frequently run off on their own, particularly in country areas, and generally return home unharmed within a few hours. If, however, you lose your dog on a walk and are concerned, stay where you are and call many times. The dog's power of scent and hearing is so strong that it may well find you, even if it is several miles away.

You may find that, in due course, the dog has returned to your house or car anyway. If not, return at dusk or early morning to the place where you lost the dog. Again call several times and then be prepared to wait quietly. If the dog is frightened, it may take some time before approaching you.

Dog stealing is not uncommon nowadays and if your dog has failed to return after, say 24 hours, consider contacting police stations, dogs' homes, veterinary surgeons and similar organizations. Prepare a written description of the dog and accompany it, ideally, with a photograph.

Grooming

A young puppy must get used to being groomed regularly, even though it may, at first, have little coat. Lay the puppy on a table or on your lap for a few minutes while brushing and combing the coat, clipping the nails and cleaning eyes and ears, if necessary. Not only is this good discipline for the pup which learns to submit to its owner's wishes at this early stage but it also accustoms it to the regular routine of grooming which, with many breeds, will be a daily, life-long factor.

In addition, it is useful to accustom the dog to pill-taking during these early days. Using a vitamin tablet, tiny piece of biscuit or other morsel of tablet size, open the dog's mouth and put the pill on the back of the tongue. Close the dog's mouth and stroke the throat until the pill is swallowed. Performed regularly, this becomes a habit so that when the dog needs medication, there will be no difficulties.

If your dog has special grooming needs, arrange a visit to the breeder when the dog's coat is more fully grown. Ask to be shown exactly how it should be groomed. Alternatively, veterinary staff can probably advise on how best to look after the dog's coat and what tools are needed. If your breed needs professional trimming, breed clubs or veterinary surgeons can advise on skilled and experienced trimmers, many of whom will make home visits.

Coat shedding can be a problem on carpets and furniture. The best way to deal with this is to remove as much as possible of the coat outdoors. Using a rubber glove, repeatedly stroke the dog from head to tail, removing handfuls of hair as you do so. Once this dead hair is removed, the new coat will grow much quicker.

Exercise

The Ratings Chart of Popular Dog Breeds shows clearly that the exercise needs of dogs vary greatly from breed to breed. Toy dogs need comparatively little in the way of organized walks, while working and hunting dogs need a great deal of activity in order to remain both physically and psychologically fit. Also, the amount of exercise a dog needs varies from individual to individual and with experience you will be able to gauge just how much your particular dog needs and enjoys. Remember that all dogs need exercise of some kind and that you must be able to provide this *on a regular basis*, whether the needs be minimal, moderate or extensive. Most dogs need daily exercise, and strenuous weekend activity is no replacement, especially if the dog has been confined indoors in close quarters for most of the week. Even small dogs need to run about and play regularly, although a daily walk may not be essential.

Many owners of medium-sized and larger breeds take their dog along when jogging or cycling and this is an excellent way of building up the dog/owner relationship. In urban areas, however, the dog must be traffic-wise and quick to respond to its owner's commands in case of danger or difficulty. It is also important not to overdo either the speed or length of jogging or cycling exercises so as to exhaust the dog.

Beagle puppy in kennel

Boarding kennels

There are times in a dog's life when it must be left in the care of people other than its owner, although ideally these times should be few. Whether its owner is on holiday or vacation, a business trip or even, say, in hospital, the dog must be cared for by willing (and dog-loving) relatives or friends or alternatively put into a boarding kennel. Ideally, the dog should stay in the environment with which it is familiar – that is, its home – with a friend or relative as house-sitter, following the routine of care, exercise and grooming that has already been established. Never leave a dog alone in the house with the promise of visits from neighbours. A dog needs lots of human company and it is preferable to take the dog to the house of a relative or friend, although this may be slightly disturbing for some dogs. However, this is not always practical for some and, moreover, many dog owners feel that a boarding kennel is a better alternative, since the dog will be well cared for by people who are knowledgeable about dogs.

The best way to find a boarding kennel is by recommendation from other pet owners. Start your research early as the best ones get booked up as quickly as a popular hotel does. If possible, send the dog for a weekend before you go away for a longer time, to see how it takes to boarding and to instill the idea that you will come back to collect it. Expect to comply with kennel rules about vaccinations, etc and to show the certificates signed by a veterinary surgeon. Make sure you collect and deliver the dog at the agreed times if you want to be a popular client. Few kennels will take puppies under six months to board, and they are wary of taking very old dogs which may be greatly disturbed by changes in food and routine and the inevitable noise. At both ends of the dog's life, the devoted owner makes other arrangements or else stays at home for the sake of the dog.

BREEDING FROM YOUR DOG

Most responsible dog owners choose to have their pet dogs desexed since unplanned or careless breeding not only impairs the purity of dog breeds but also adds to the thousands of pitiful, abandoned dogs in an already over-populated world. It is important to think very carefully before you decide to allow either your male or female dog to breed.

Siring a litter

Male dogs are capable of siring a litter from about 10 months old, yet few well-kept dogs ever have this opportunity unless a mistake occurs or the dog has been successful in the show ring and is therefore in demand as a stud animal. It is generally unwise to allow a household pet to be put to stud, however tempting the chance. Once back in your home, the dog may display considerable disturbance and frustration, leading him to wander in search of bitches, to urine-mark his territory both inside and out and in other ways to challenge your authority in an effort to achieve dominance. Having once mated with a bitch, the dog will attempt to do so again and this will be a constant worry for the owner unless the dog is castrated. Champion stud dogs living in kennels have a regular flow of bitches coming to them, so that similar problems do not arise.

Male sexual behaviour

Many males go through a time of heightened sexual activity at around 12-18 months when they will mount furniture and people's legs in imitation of mating a bitch. This behaviour should be curbed in the same way that you would any other inappropriate action by the dog. In most cases, the hormone stimulation will soon subside and the dog will give no more offence. Where the behaviour persists, as it does sometimes in small terriers, consult a veterinary surgeon who may suggest castration or reducing the hormone imbalance by medication.

Great Dane mother and puppy

Considerations before breeding a litter

There are too many puppies looking for homes to add to their numbers lightly, so do consult with your family, breeder and veterinary surgeon before deciding to breed from your bitch. One of the major considerations is the time, expense and effort involved in rearing a litter which will tie you to your home and the pups for approximately four months.

- Check with the veterinary surgeon and the breeder that your bitch is sound enough in health and temperament to be bred from. Never breed from any bitch with a major health or temperament defect, since it is unfair on owners of the next generation.

- If a toy breed, ask if the dog is large enough to bear a litter easily.

- Has your house enough space for whelping and rearing puppies?

- Remembering that growing puppies can destroy household furnishings and your garden.

- Can you afford the expense of whelping and rearing puppies? Consider, among other things, that the puppies may not survive to be sold and that the bitch may need an expensive Caesarian operation.

- Will you be able to sell the pups if you are not a regular breeder with an established reputation?

- Have you the time, skill and patience to interview prospective buyers and the ability to refuse if they cannot offer a satisfactory home?

- Will you be able to run puppies on until four months or so if unsold?

- Are you prepared to take back a puppy or dog months, or even years, later if the owner is unable to keep it? This is the breeder's moral duty.

- Do not consider deliberately breeding from a mongrel since the puppies have no assured future.

Bitch's breeding cycle

A bitch can only be bred from when she is in oestrus, (in season or on heat). This occurs for the first time at between six and 18 months old, large breeds tending to be the latest. The heat period reoccurs nominally at six-monthly intervals but more generally it is an interval of eight to 10 months, or even longer, depending on the individual. Bitches are not bred from until at least their second season, or when they are over two years old. Coming into season is characterized by:

- Increased excitement, fussy behaviour, or nervousness, according to the individual.

- Enlargement of the vulva (the external genital organ) up to 2-3 times its normal size.

- A bloodstained discharge from the vulva. The first day this appears marks the first day of "the season", in dog breeder parlance.

The bitch continues to discharge blood, sometimes in significant quantities, for 10 to 16 days, possibly longer. When the bloodstained discharge stops, this usually indicates that the bitch is ready to be mated with a dog, although this is not necessarily so. When the time for mating approaches, the bitch will be eager to reach a dog, so keep very close control over her, not even leaving her alone in the garden. Male dogs will have shown interest in the bitch long before this and will make a nuisance of themselves around your home if the owners do not control them. It is very important to keep all male dogs away from the bitch at this time, whether they are related or not and whatever their breed or size. You may also find increased territory markings by males inside and outside your property.

You should already have made arrangements with an experienced stud dog. Be guided by its owner on how to proceed with the planned mating. Once the peak of the season (11-16 days) has passed, your bitch will become progressively less attractive to dogs, the vulva will shrink in size and her behaviour will become calm and normal. Towards the end of the season, give her a good bath to remove scents which may cling to her coat.

Pregnancy in the bitch lasts from 57-70 days, with the majority of puppies being born at about 63 days from the day of mating. Giving birth in the purebred bitch is not always easy and you will be wise to take instruction from a breeder and/or veterinary surgeon on how to prepare and what to expect.

Phantom pregnancy

The hormones of the bitch's breeding cycle act in the same way whether she is mated or not. For this reason, your bitch may simulate all the physical and mental stages of an actual pregnancy without mating. In phantom pregnancy, the bitch may come into milk, have an enlarged abdomen, make a whelping nest and attempt to nurture plastic toys or other inanimate objects. The intensity of the phantom pregnancy varies from individual to individual, but some bitches go through severe changes in temperament.

Treat the condition with firmness, not sympathy. Remove all toys or objects she may treat as puppies, cut down on her food, and give more brisk exercise to divert her interest. In extreme cases, you may need to consult the vet for medication to help hormone adjustment and to dry up the milk. The only permanent treatment for phantom pregnancy is to have the bitch spayed.

Coping with the season

Preparations are sold, such as liquids, sprays and tablets which are said to disguise the smell of a bitch in heat. They are all useless and a waste of money since male dogs can always scent out a bitch in season. If at all possible, keep the bitch within your own property for the duration of the heat; she will come to no harm from lack of exercise for this time. Pet shops can provide bolts and pads to save the bitch's discharge from staining furnishings.

Contraception

Developments from the human birth pill are available in tablet or injection form which will keep the bitch from coming into season, either temporarily or more or less permanently if the treatment is repeated. Discuss the matter with your veterinary surgeon well before the bitch's first season.

The ultimate and most successful contraceptive is to have the bitch spayed. This is a major but relatively safe operation done in every veterinary surgery almost daily. The bitch recovers very quickly, although some vets like to keep a bitch in their own care for one night. Owners fear that the spayed bitch will become fat but, although weight gain is easier in a neutered animal, increased exercise and a little less food should keep the bitch's weight down. Some breeds, notably the Spaniels, grow a very thick almost ungroomable coat after spaying but this is one of the drawbacks which you must weigh up against the nuisance of an in-season bitch. Consult both the breeder and the vet before coming to a conclusion.

Mismating

If your bitch mates by accident and you fear she is pregnant, there are three alternative courses of action.

- Take her to the veterinary surgeon for a hormone injection within 36 hours of the mating. This will bring her back to the start of her season and you will have to be more careful with her the next time. The injection is not without risk of serious illness to the bitch and should not be undertaken lightly.

- An alternative is to take a bitch for a pregnancy diagnosis three weeks after the mating. This is the earliest time a veterinary surgeon can give an opinion on whether she is pregnant. If she is, she can be spayed at this time.

- Let the pregnancy proceed and cull the litter to the minimal number of pups to take care of the milk. When making this decision, remember that in a small breed the birth may be exceedingly difficult if the sire was much larger.

It takes time and patience to educate a puppy in basic good behaviour and to accustom it to different situations and many types of people. Activities with your puppy early on in its development should include familiarizing it with traffic noise and with varying types of floor or ground surfaces. It is equally important to socialize a puppy so that it is used to encountering both very old and young people, as well as other dogs and household pets. Remember, when training your puppy, that it relies on hearing and scent, more so than sight, to give it information about its immediate world. A dog, for example, can scent out an individual who is afraid of dogs, however well he or she may conceal it, and will be wary of or hostile to that person. Similarly, it may misinterpret the boisterous cries and shouts of young children unless accustomed to these early on. However, once your dog has been taught basic good behaviour, there are a number of other pleasurable activities which can be engaged in.

Show ring
At the highest level, "showing" your dog can be an expensive, time-consuming, albeit absorbing hobby. Your dog must be registered with your national kennel club and conform to the breed standards laid down by the club. If you have ambitions to introduce your dog to the demanding world of the show ring, consult your breeder first for a friendly and informal opinion about its chances of success.

Obedience training
You may decide to take your dog's education to a higher level and to enrol in obedience training classes, should your breed of dog excel at this activity. If you and your dog are promising material, you may progress to competition level or be a member of a display team. Like showing, engaging in top-level obedience trials requires a lot of commitment and this is only for the serious enthusiast.

Agility games

Agility competitions are one of the newest activities for companion dogs of all breeds and crossbreeds. Even if you never aspire to public competition, agility can be an excellent game for family and dog, providing enthusiasm does not outrun common sense and the dog is not extended beyond its capabilities. One of the greatest deprivations of even the best kept companion dog is the lack of freedom to run about and exercise its natural talents and inclinations. Walks are fine exercise, but miles of tramping on hard roads is hardly a great pleasure for owner or animal. Instead, think about providing a playground in your garden which can amuse your children as well. Even a medium-sized lawn can make a good agility course, which will give your dog hours of entertainment and also lead to a fitter and more obedient dog.

Agility games should not start until the dog is 12 months old or even older for very heavy breeds, and obviously, such activity is unsuitable for the old dog or one suffering from deteriorating sight or other disability. It is unwise to encourage your dog to jump obstacles if your garden is not well-fenced, otherwise you may be programming it to get out and wander. The important part of the agility game is that the handler runs alongside the dog, encouraging it over and through obstacles but not jumping with it. Before agility training can begin, the dog must be perfect at basic commands such as sit, stay and come when called.

Start teaching the dog while on the lead to jump a low 10cm (4 inch) log from one direction and then the other. Gradually raise the height of the jump to a maximum of 75cm (2 feet 6 inches). Small breeds enjoy the activity as much as large breeds, but you will need to scale down the obstacles. The next stage is to get the dog to jump on command when off the lead, with the handler running alongside. "Over" is the most practical command. If both dog and owner enjoy agility, the next step is to construct jumps from waste timber, and gradually lay out a proper course. Allow the dog several strides between each obstacle. As well as long and high jumps, dogs can negotiate a row of alternating poles, climb ladders, walk down planks, jump through a suspended tyre, and wriggle through a cloth tunnel (a groundsheet loosely anchored to the ground will do for beginners).

If you wish, progress to one of the many dog clubs which teach agility on sophisticated courses and enter teams in local or national competition. At this level, speed is also important, so dog and handler need to memorize the course and be quick and accurate at obstacles. Agility is a great game or sport, depending on the level to which the owner wants to take it. Those who have plenty of patience and who like teaching dogs can find it a fascinating hobby.

Competing in agility trials

Charitable work

All the animal charities need sensible help, either with day-to-day manual work or with fund raising. You could take part in or help to organize many enjoyable events. Sponsored walks with dogs are a popular way of raising money and an excellent way of meeting other dog-owning people. Rescue organizations will also welcome your help. You could be invaluable at picking up dogs and driving them to new homes, or taking them into your own home to test their suitability for rehousing.

A gentler occupation is to visit retirement homes, long-stay hospital wards and schools with your dog. This idea is gaining popularity since the opportunity to stroke a pet, and talk about dogs is much valued by people deprived of their own pets. You will make new friends and find that your visits are eagerly anticipated. Obviously for this work, you must have an outgoing and friendly dog kept in spotless condition. In the US, pet rooms have been organized in many general hospitals, so that patients recovering from illnesses may spend a little time with their own pet without upsetting those who are not fond of animals. Offer to set up such a service in your local hospital and to carry it through immaculately.

Numbers in bold type refer to main text entries. Numbers in italics refer to illustration captions.